MASTERS OF METAL

MASTERS OF METAL

Lee Martyn

Exclusively Distributed
In North America By

Cherry Lane Books

PORT CHESTER, NY 10573

DEDICATION

For Katie Victoria and Jessica Louise

Cherry Lane Books
Port Chester, NY 10573, USA

First Published in Great Britain in 1984 By Zomba
Books, Zomba House, 165–167 Willesden High Road,
London NW10 2SG

© Lee Martyn, 1984

ISBN 0 946391 48 3

Designed by Jim Reader

CoverDesigned by The Fish Family

Edited by Peter Hogan

Production Services by Book Production Consultants,
Cambridge

Typeset by Wenden Typesetting Services Limited,
Wenden Court, Wendens Ambo, Saffron Walden, Essex

Printed by Bemrose Printing C.I.P., Derby

First Edition

Contents

Also available in the same series are:

Van Halen
Ozzy Osbourne
Eurythmics
Culture Club
Iron Maiden

The above books can be ordered from:

Zomba Books
165–167 Willesden High Rd
London NW10 2SG

OR

Cherry Lane Books
Port Chester
NY 10573
New York
United States of America

Introduction

The late sixties were a good time to be growing up. At school the tedium of lessons was broken by lunch-times spent listening to the standard-issue school record player in the art block, volume turned up as loud as we could bear, while Steppenwolf, Blue Cheer, Grand Funk, Cream, and, of course, Hendrix, played a whole new kind of music – the first *real* music, we thought. It was heavily-amplified, melodic but not too harmonic, and the bass-drum combination sounded like a Panzer division blitzkrieging the countryside. And over and above everything else there was the guitar sound, whether enhanced by wah-wah effects or feedback, or just played fast and neat with no frills. The guitar was the thing. We all wanted to be guitar heroes, formed our own bands, acted as anti-social as our heroes, grew our hair long, cultivated a shabby appearance and generally upset our parents.

It was simply hard rock in those days. Heavy Metal as a category didn't really exist, but even then some of us knew that this much heavier, perhaps cruder, musical form was *real* rock music – all the rest was somehow insipid, lacking in energy. 'Purple Haze', 'Badge', 'Born To Be Wild' (with the prophetic line, "Heavy Metal thunder") these were our models for the future of rock music. And in the next few years – 1969–70 we're talking about here! – it seemed as though the earth had opened up and thrown out its riches. *Led Zeppelin I* and *II, Deep Purple In Rock* and *Black Sabbath*: these albums set the parameters for the new music, and between them provided all the elements from which Heavy Metal was to grow. The riffs, the guitar virtuosi, the prominence of the vocals (usually high-pitched) and a firm belief in playing it LOUD.

As this book proves, regardless of the music press, Heavy Metal didn't die in the mid-Seventies and wasn't re-born in 1979 when the New Wave of British Heavy Metal arrived; it was simply neglected by the rock magazines, who, jaded and out of touch, buried the kicking corpse. Or tried to. The albums still kept going gold, the tours kept selling out, the new heavy rock bands kept on appearing (AC/DC, Def Leppard, Motorhead et al . . .). Which is not to say that in Heavy Metal, as in all forms of music, there isn't a certain amount of derivative rubbish, simply to counter that tiresomely repeated accusation in the press that "It all sounds the same." You would have thought that a bunch of middle-aged halfwits had taken over the rock establishment – critics who thought that energy was the sole prerogative of new wave punk bands, and musical skill limited to the emerging synthesiser hordes . . . musical ability and high octane energy was to be found *thriving* in the Heavy Metal community.

Nonetheless, the early eighties have witnessed a resurgence of interest in heavy rock and Heavy Metal. If the audience for Heavy Metal was healthy in the late Seventies, it's phenomenal in the Eighties. Gold albums were replaced by platinum, moderately successful bands of long-standing became 'over-night' stars – the Scorpions, for instance – and at long last the field began to develop its own magazines (*Kerrang!* in particular) and win radio airplay. Those of us who gathered about the old school record player all those years ago aren't surprised in the least. We always knew it would happen; as Shakespeare's Hamlet was heard to say; "Here's metal more attractive."

AC/DC

In the face of growing sophistication the rock music scene in the Seventies seemed to lose touch with its roots, its essence. The hard, gutsy energy that gave rock its cutting edge seemed suddenly in very short supply. Yet even as rock music seemed on its last legs in America and Britain, down in Albert Studios in Sydney, Australia, a band of young hopefuls were cutting their first album – high energy, hard rock that sounded like a cross between Chuck Berry and the Stones at their best. It was 1975, and that album, *High Voltage*, and its successor, *T.N.T.* launched AC/DC in their homeland, with sales of over 100,000 copies apiece. A year later the two albums were amalgamated as *High Voltage* for the American and UK markets. AC/DC's conquest of the world had begun.

AC/DC began life as a school band, formed by guitarist Malcolm Young in 1973. Dissatisfied with a three-piece line-up, Malcolm recruited his sixteen-year-old brother Angus as lead guitarist, and reorganised the group, bringing in Phil Rudd on drums and Mark Evans on bass before discovering the perfect vocalist for the group in Bon Scott. Scott had suffered a car crash in 1974 and was at first the group's van driver and roadie before fronting the band with Angus. The group's distinctive sound and image were thus formulated before they went into big brother George Young's recording studios to cut their first album.

AC/DC have always been a hard-working live band, carrying out gruelling tours where every concert taxed them to the limit. Angus, distinctive in schoolboy short trousers, tie, jacket, cap and satchel, never stops, whether leaping from precariously-balanced speaker stacks, strutting about the stage like something demented, or lying on his back to peel off a blistering guitar solo. Beside him, Bon Scott was his perfect complement: bare-chested, cloth cap on his head, with gruff, throaty vocals and sexually-suggestive antics making it quite clear what songs like "The Jack" (a song about VD) were *really* all about. And behind those two were Malcolm and the rhythm section, providing the gut energy that the band is renowned for. Live, AC/DC are brash, violent and exciting: an excitement that they've rarely failed to capture on vinyl as well as on stage.

Their first tour of the UK, which started in April 1976, was a taste of things to come. They supported Back Street Crawler, and blew them off stage. Meanwhile, the compilation album *High Voltage*, had been released to general critical acclaim, though in those early days of punk the music press was looking elsewhere for the stars of tomorrow. A second UK tour followed, this time with AC/DC alone on the bill; a tour which won them a hard core of fans in Britain. Then came a 19-date tour supporting Ritchie Blackmore's Rainbow throughout Europe. Back in the UK

again they played a further 15 dates, including the Reading Festival. Word was getting round, and it was only mid-September. Their hard-working, hard rock approach seemed to be paying off. Yet their major headlining tour of the UK in late 1976 proved overambitious; the music was good and the fans more enthusiastic than ever, but they failed to fill the larger venues.

Dirty Deeds Done Dirt Cheap, their second UK album was released to coincide with the tour and, for once, was a disappointment. It had its high points – 'Big Balls', 'Rocker' and 'Problem Child' – but was otherwise muted. It lacked the raw-edged power that fans and critics had come to expect.

But AC/DC were undaunted. Fresh challenges awaited them; in particular, the States. October found them touring the clubs in America, getting good reviews and selling a few copies of *High Voltage*, their only US album. Again, it was a start. An intimation of what was to come.

In early 1977 they recorded *Let There Be Rock* (released worldwide in June). It was, and is, AC/DC on top form,

typified by the classic track, 'Whole Lotta Rosie' – infectious, high voltage rock 'n' roll. The whole album was ferociously aggressive and, played live during their February/March tour of the UK (fresh from the studios) it confirmed them as the best of the upcoming heavy acts.

Spring 1977 saw them supporting Black Sabbath on their European tour, and that Summer they toured the States on an exhaustive schedule, establishing a hard core following that, in the coming years, was to swell to massive proportions. Before that Stateside tour bassist Mark Evans quit, and ex-Home Bassist Cliff Williams stepped in.

Firmly established on both sides of the Atlantic and viewed as cult heroes in their own country, AC/DC were ready to take the next step. 1978 saw a new studio album, *Powerage*, released in April. It was just as aggressive, if not downright vicious, as its predecessor, and in October that year came another classic album, the live *If You Want Blood – You've Got It*, fifty two minutes of brutal heavy rock which makes the Stones look meek.

Up to the end of 1978 each album had done progressively better in terms of sales and, because of their willingness to take the music to their fans – their unrelenting energy – they were on the verge of becoming one of the world's major music acts. *Highway To Hell*, released in July 1979, went platinum in the States and climbed to No 17 in the charts.

Tours, albums, the unrelenting climb to the top; all of this seemed suddenly checked on February 21st 1980 when Bon Scott was found dead in his car, after having choked on his own vomit. For a time it seemed that AC/DC might not continue, but then in April they announced that they had a new singer, Brian Johnson, formerly of Geordie, and the release of *Back In Black* in July proved Johnson to be an able replacement for the sadly missed Scott. The album went to No 3 in the US charts and eventually sold more than 8 million copies worldwide. AC/DC were suddenly, if not surprisingly, the biggest Heavy Metal act around.

1981 saw them release *For Those About To Rock We Salute You*, a multi-platinum earner in the States as well as their first No 1 album. AC/DC-fever was at high pitch. Earlier in the year the *Dirty Deeds Done Dirt Cheap* album was finally released in the US, five years after it was recorded, and went immediately to No 3 in the charts there.

After years of non-stop activity, AC/DC took a rest in 1982. Their albums were all going gold and platinum worldwide, but *For Those About To Rock*, with its impressive, anthemic title track, seemed for a time to be the last word from AC/DC. Then, in the Autumn of 1983 *Flick Of The Switch* was released, coincidental with the announcement that Phil Judd was being replaced on drums by 20-year old Simon Wright. With new material and renewed enthusiasm the bad boys of boogie are touring once more, making brains shake throughout the world. Wann'a tell you a story . . .

Albums:

High Voltage (Australia only) (1975)   *T.N.T.* (Australia only) (1975)   *High Voltage* (1976)★   *Dirty Deeds Done Dirt Cheap* (1976) (US, 1981)   *Let There Be Rock* (1977)   *Powerage* (1978)   *If You Want Blood, You've Got It* (1978)   *Highway To Hell* (1979)   *Back In Black* (1980)   *For Those About To Rock* (1981)   *Flick Of The Switch* (1983)

★ Compilation album

Aerosmith

Aerosmith have their origins in the summer of 1970 when three musicians from the New Hampshire area got together to play the club and bar circuit. 22-year old Steve Tyler was the drummer, 19-year old Joe Perry the guitarist and 18-year old Tom Hamilton the bassist. After a while Tyler quit and Joey Kramer came in on drums. A second guitarist was recruited in 18-year old Brad Whitford. Then, ousted from his drum role but still keen to partake in the band's music, Tyler returned, this time as vocalist. Aerosmith took flight.

As fledgling rockers the youthful Aerosmith paid their dues the hard way, playing not merely clubs and bars, but high schools and colleges as well – at first in New Hampshire, then later in 1970, in the Boston area, where the band based itself for the next year and a half. But the hard slog seemed ultimately unrewarding, and only an introduction to management team David Krebs and Steve Leber got them out of their rut. They began to play odd gigs in New York, at one of which – at Max's Kansas City – they were seen by Columbia executive Clive Davis, who was impressed enough with what he saw to sign them to his label.

Their early survival ploy of gig-gig-gig remained an essential part of Aerosmith's success story, for it was by constantly touring to support each album as it came out, that Aerosmith rose to their place among the top rank American heavy bands. Theirs was a blues-based hard rock style that sometimes had an unexpected lyrical delicacy. An example of this is 'Dream On' from their debut album, *Aerosmith*, released in June 1973. It made little impact as a single on its first release, but eventually reached No 6 in the US charts in February 1976 (and stayed in the top forty 11 weeks) when reissued.

Steve Tyler's vocals, reminiscent of a cross between Paul Simon and Demis Roussos, were a perfect complement to Joe Perry's guitar phrasing and the two became Aerosmith's strongest songwriters, penning numbers like 'Walk This Way' and 'Back In The Saddle'. But it was the raunchy rhythm section that gave the band its distinctive sound. *Get Your Wings* (the reference is to a Hells Angels ritual) was released in March 1974 and confirmed that the band were one of the hottest new acts on the US circuit, the dirty-rock sound of 'Same Old Song And Dance' being heard nationwide as Aerosmith toured coast to coast, belting out one of the hottest (and loudest) rock acts around. The success of their policy can be gauged by the fact that the album eventually went platinum, though not until after their next album had been released . . . *Toys In The Attic.*

It was late '75 and 'Sweet Emotion', from the *Toys In The Attic* album was No. 36 in the singles chart – an ultra-

heavy number that was typical of Aerosmith's stage set. The album, eagerly awaited by a host of 'Smith fans, charted at once – and stayed. For almost two years it could be found somewhere in the top half of the US album charts. Platinum? Of course. In fact, 'Walk This Way' from *Toys In The Attic* was yet another case of second-time lucky for Aerosmith, the single getting to No. 11 in the charts on its re-issue in December 1976. And in between times Aerosmith had cut what was by far their heaviest album yet, *Rocks*. A succinct review of the album, released in the summer of 1976, would read 'It *does*, doesn't it!" Aerosmith had shed the lyricism of 'Dream On', and replaced it with 100% heavy rocking. 'Last Child' (No. 21 in June '76) and 'Back In The Saddle' (No. 38 in May '77) were the two hits from the album. Yet strangely enough, the days of Aerosmith's popularity were numbered.

The band had not ceased touring since their formation in 1970. They weren't the kind of group to take months in the studio and ages rehearsing their songs – the new material was cast and polished on the road, and when the group was tired from its constantly crowded itinery the material suffered. Early '77 saw them exhausted, physically and creatively. They took several months rest, then returned to the studio to record their next album.

Draw The Line, released in the summer of 1977, was perhaps something of a disappointment after earlier efforts and was less enthusiastically received by the fans. Even so, Aerosmith were still one of the biggest rock acts in the USA (alongside Kiss) in terms of popularity and the album was platinum within a month of its release. But the rot was setting in. Joe Perry was beginning to feel uncomfortable in the band, and their decision to play the villains in Robert Stigwood's movie, *Sgt. Pepper's Lonely Hearts Club Band*, was questionable to say the least. Even so, one good thing came out of that – their version of the Beatles' 'Come Together', which reached No. 23 in the singles charts in September 1978.

All of 1977 and most of '78 saw Aerosmith out of the public eye; mainly because their two month rest had extended into a permanent lay-off from touring. When they returned the big crowds were still there, and there was still a huge audience for their 1979 live double album, *Live! Bootleg*, but the old magic had gone. Joe Perry, his discontent with the band having come to a pitch, quit the band that year, and was followed in 1980 by guitarist, Brad Whitford, who had stayed long enough to see their 1979 album, *Night In The Ruts* earn its predictable platinum disc. But there were no more hit singles, no more sell-out tours, and new men Jimmy Crespo (guitar) and Rick Dufay did nothing to recapture the old spirit of Aerosmith. They appear on the 1982 album, *Rock In A Hard Place*, but then were gone from the group who seemed, after a decade as one of America's top bands, to have finally given up the ghost.

But as with Black Sabbath and Deep Purple, one could say of Aerosmith, "Rumours of the band's decease are premature", for in the Spring of 1984 it was announced that Aerosmith were back together again – Tyler, Kramer, Hamilton, Whitford and Perry. The old hot-rocking five-piece from New Hampshire were back and raring to go. A 30-City US tour was lined up for mid-summer 1984 and material for a new album was being prepared. Which is not to say that the old songs won't get an airing – in fact Aerosmith are busy re-vamping their old hits ready for the road. And if they've anything like the power they had back in the heydays of 75–77, then they're likely to blow most of the new wave of American Heavy Metal bands off the stage! Not only that, but European and British Aerosmith fans, deprived of seeing the band for so long now, will get the opportunity sometime in '85 if present plans come to fruition.

(Oh, and by the way, did you know that Eddie Van Halen also started in the club circuit . . . playing Aerosmith songs.)

Albums:
Aerosmith (1973) *Get Your Wings* (1974) *Toys In The Attic* (1975) *Rocks* (1976) *Draw The Line* (1977) *Live! Bootleg* (1979) *Night In The Ruts* (1979) *Aerosmith's Greatest Hits* (1980)* *Rock In A Hard Place* (1982) *Rock Giants* (1982)*

* Compilation albums.

PHOTO: L.F.I./PAUL COX

April Wine

Nova Scotia, Canada was the birthplace of April Wine, one of North America's more popular heavy bands. The group was the brainchild of 18-year old Myles Goodwyn, whose talented guitar playing and ear for a good song soon won the band a recording deal with a Canadian label, Big Tree; their first album, *April Wine*, appeared in 1970.

The first few years of April Wine's existence were marked by sudden and frequent personnel changes, as Goodwyn sought the right musicians to play what was essentially his own personal brand of Heavy Metal (tuneful, harmonic, yet with teeth!). He moved the group to Montreal, where they've been based ever since, and cut a second album, *On Record*, in 1971. Then, in the Spring of 1972, the band had a big success with the single, 'You Could Have Been A Lady', which was a top twenty hit in Canada and, more importantly, went to No. 32 in the US singles charts. Featured on the 1973 album, *Electric Jewels*, it showed that April Wine had a gentler side.

1973 saw the beginnings of a more stable line-up as Gary Moffat joined the band as a second guitarist and Jerry Mercer settled in as April Wine's drummer. These two

featured on 1974's *Live* album. Then, in early 1975, bassist Steve Lang was recruited. The immediate result was the much heavier sound of *Stand Back* (the first of many albums produced by Myles Goodwyn), which went platinum in Canada.

By the mid-Seventies April wine were in the not-so-unusual position of being huge in their own country and yet virtual unknowns elsewhere. Every new record released in Canada was immediate gold, with *The Whole World's Going Crazy* (1976) and *Live At The El Mocambo* (1977) earning the band platinum discs. They were reasonably well known in the United States, of course, but Britain, Europe and Japan, which traditionally welcomed heavy groups, were strangely ignored by the band.

In 1977 Brian Greenway joined the band as third guitarist and backing vocalist, completing their present day line-up. The band signed with Capitol worldwide in 1978 and released a new studio album for their new label in 1979. *First Glance* spawned a new hit single, 'Roller', which climbed to No. 34 in the US singles charts in April

1979. *Harder . . . Faster*, their 1980 release, lived up to its name but still didn't break them to a larger audience. That year also saw the band touring the UK for the first time and looking to wider audiences for their clear, hard sound.

A decade's hard work finally paid off in 1981 with the release of *The Nature Of The Beast*. It was the band's first big-selling album in the States, earning them a gold disc, and the single from the album, 'Just Between You And Me' reached No. 21 in the US charts in March 1981.

Two further albums have come from the band since *The Nature Of The Beast* and neither has been anything like as successful. *Power Play*. their 1982 release, was frankly a disappointment, but *Animal Grace*, their 1984 album, saw the band back on form.

Thirteen albums on and it seems that April Wine are no more. In May 1984 Myles Goodwyn was recording his first solo album and saying openly that the band was defunct. Although at present it's only a rumour, if it proves to be true (and without songwriter/guitarist/singer/producer Goodwyn, April Wine aren't really a going concern) then their live act can at least still be seen on their video, *Live In Concert*, recorded in London in the early 1980s.

Albums:

April Wine (1970) *On Record* (1971) *Electric Jewels* (1973) *Live* (1974) *Stand Back* (1975) *The Whole World's Going Crazy* (1976) *For Ever For Now* (1976) *Live At The El Mocambo* (1977) *First Glance* (1979) *Harder . . . Faster* (1980) *The Nature Of The Beast* (1981) *Power Play* (1982) *Animal Grace* (1984)

Pat Benatar

Patricia Andrezejewski was born in Brooklyn, New York in 1953, daughter of a sheet metal worker, and grew up on Long Island. Her Catholic upbringing was unexceptional, though she did shine at both physical fitness classes and at singing. Her teachers, impressed by her early ability, made her pursue the latter, with a career in opera in view. She spent a year studying vocal training – a year's hard work preparing her for the prestigious Juilliard School Of Music. She enrolled, but was appalled by the rigid disciplines of the School and quit almost before she had begun. She dropped out and married her high school sweetheart, Dennis Benatar.

Eighteen-year-old Pat Benatar, housewife and bank clerk, lived in Virginia for a time with her husband, who was in the army. Realising that she was getting in a rut, she began studying for a career in health education, paying for her course by taking a job as a singing waitress at the Raging 20s Club in Hopewell, Virginia, singing cover versions of top 40 hits while dressed in a food-stained leopard-skin outfit. This was only a minor improvement, yet it impressed on Pat where her future direction lay, and in 1975 Pat and her husband moved back to New York where, broke and depressed, she tried to break into the cabaret circuit of Manhattan. It was at this time that her first real break came. She entered a talent contest at the Catch A Rising Star club, owned by Rick Newman. She had a rotten billing, coming on stage at 2.45 in the morning, but still managed to impress everyone there, including Newman, who was to become her manager.

Between 1975 and 1978 Pat Benatar worked the club circuit and got a band together. Husband Dennis was divorced and guitarist/keyboards player Neil Geraldo entered her life as both band organiser and boyfriend (they married in 1982). Also in the band were Scott St.Clair Sheets on guitar, Roger Capps on bass and Myron Grombacher on drums. From the start what they were playing was far heavier than the normal club material, and under Newman's and Geraldo's influence she shed the Streisand/Ross influences in her music altogether and became an out-and-out raunchy rock'n'roller.

In 1979 Newman got her a recording contract, and late in the year her debut album, *In The Heat Of The Night* made its appearance. The best cut on the album was perhaps John Cougar's song, 'I Need A Lover', but as Cougar's own version was in the charts, Benatar released something else from the album as a single. That something else was 'Heartbreaker', and by February 1980 it was at No. 23 in the US singles chart. Another single, 'We Live For Love' followed in May and reached No. 27, while the album edged its way up onto the borders of the Top Twenty and went gold. Both the music and the image were just right for

the times, the band's subtle, imaginative heavy rock and Pat's dynamic vocals blending superbly. Pat Benatar clones started appearing in their thousands about the country as she slowly became the USA's top female rocker.

October 1980 saw a second album in the shops and a new single heading up the charts. 'Hit Me With Your Best Shot' got to No. 9 and stayed high in the charts for fifteen weeks. Meanwhile *Crimes Of Passion*, an uncompromising rocker of an album, went up to No. 2 in the albums chart, kept from the top spot only by Lennon's *Double Fantasy*. The platinum discs went up on the wall, and Pat Benatar took her show on the road, spawning lookalikes wherever she went. In just two years she had fulfilled her musical ambitions, and everyone was asking "What next?"

Precious Time, released in 1981, was, in retrospect, guaranteed to go platinum and get to No. 1 in the albums chart, which it did almost immediately. There had been another top twenty hit earlier in the year with 'Treat Me Right', but two more singles from the new album made an impact in the charts, 'Fire and Ice' (No. 17) and 'Shadows Of The Night', a better song, perhaps, but less popular. *Precious Time* saw the band's style maturing and moving away from heaviness towards a more melodic, more commercial rock format. It also coincided with the greatest media interest in Pat Benatar. There was a definitive Pat Benatar 'look', a kind of chic and sexy new wave look that suggested aggressive femininity: the kind of modern young woman who could cope very well for herself. But the pressures on the band were great at this time and they had a rough patch in 1982, Scott St.Clair Sheets leaving, to be replaced by Charlie Giordano on keyboards. Neil Geraldo moved solely to guitars and the band recorded *Get Nervous*, with its famous cover shot of Pat in a straightjacket. It was released late in 1982 and by January 1983 was No. 4 in the charts, a single from the album, 'Shadows Of The Night' having got to No. 13 the previous November.

Once again, *Get Nervous* displayed a marked movement away from the pure heaviness of the first two albums. It had its heavy moments, of course, and played live it could rock with the best of them, but it was notable that the production was toning down Benatar's rock excesses and making them more palatable for the ever-growing number of her more commercially minded fans. 'Little Too Late', a second single from the album, got to No. 20 in March 1983.

Successful, yes, but what did the critics think of ex-cabaret hopeful Pat Benatar? Quite a lot, actually. In 1980 she won the annual Grammy award for best female vocalist, then in 1981 grabbed the award again. Her brief appearance in the Debbie Harry movie, *Union City* (1981) also won her acclaim, some critics saying that her appearance was the highlight of the film. Most recently, in 1984, she won the Grammy for "Best Female Vocalist" again, even though her only recent vinyl excursion has been the *Live From Earth* album in 1983, with eight of her most famous songs played live and two new studio tracks.

There's no doubt that Pat Benatar is on the middle ground between pop-cabaret and heavy rock, yet the movement (in her words) away from "crunch rock" and towards "danceable music" hasn't totally blunted Pat Benatar's cutting edge, as the single (one of the two new tracks on *Live From Earth*) 'Love Is A Battlefield' proved. Another top twenty hit, it had all the punch of the older material plus a confidence that suggests that the best of Pat Benatar is yet to come. But then . . . well, she is quoted as saying that she wants to settle down some day and have a baby, and though her recent UK tour showed her as raunchily aggressive as ever, the slow decrease of output might indicate that she'll shortly leave the field altogether, which would be a shame. And if you want to know how much of a shame, then get hold of the video, *In Concert*, and you'll understand why millions of American schoolgirls have been mimicking her these last few years.

Albums:

In The Heat Of The Night (1979) *Crimes Of Passion* (1980) *Precious Time* (1980) *Get Nervous* (1982) *Live From Earth* (1983)

Black Sabbath

Back in 1967 four unemployed youngsters from Aston, Birmingham, formed a band called Polka Tulk. It wasn't a name that greatly appealed, even to the band, and the blues-based group changed its name to Earth, hoping to get work on the club circuit. But work was hard to come by and they were often forced to accept £10 gigs at friends' parties. Success seemed a million years away, and there's a story that at this stage two of the band were sharing one pair of shoes. But things got better – as Earth they went to Germany, working the Star Club in Hamburg (where the Beatles had been in the early 60s), playing five sets a night. From this experience the band began to change, writing its own material, including a strange, haunting, heavy piece called . . . 'Black Sabbath'.

As Black Sabbath the group at last had an identity. Bassist Geezer Butler had discovered Dennis Wheatley, the supernatural author, and the black magic influence had permeated the group's work. With this new image and new, matching material the group went into Regent Sound studios off London's Tottenham Court Road and cut their first album. It cost them £600 and most of the tracks were laid down in no more than two takes. And all on old-fashioned four-track'! The result, released by Vertigo on Friday 13th February 1970, was the album *Black Sabbath*, a flawed masterpiece that, by word of mouth alone, launched the band in their homeland. Without any publicity it reached the top ten of the album charts and stayed there. It was a new kind of music, not simply heavy, but riff-based rather than melody-based. Almost single-handedly Black Sabbath had invented a powerful new musical form – Heavy Metal.

'Evil Woman', a single from the first album did quite well, but not as well as 'Paranoid', a track recorded for their second album, which went to No. 4 in the UK charts in August 1970. They made their first tour of the States that year and on November 29th played their first session on John Peel's *Top Gear*, then the leading UK radio showcase for new progressive rock talents, playing selections from their recently issued album, *Paranoid* (which was to have been called *War Pigs* before the success of the single).

By the end of 1970 Black Sabbath were finding the black magic aura that surrounded them a hindrance (though they never wholly let it drop) and insisted it was only a gimmick. Nonetheless, they played on their dark reputation when in concert, presenting an excessively loud, almost apocalyptic set in those early years. It was a recipe for success, particularly in the States, where massive advance orders of 200,000 copies came in for their third album, *Masters Of Reality*, released in July 1971. And when *Black Sabbath Volume 4* was released in September 1972, Sabbath were alongside Deep Purple and Led Zeppelin in spearheading

Britain's heavy assault on the States. A year later came the classic *Sabbath, Bloody Sabbath*, perhaps the best album since their debut. In 1973 Black Sabbath were selling as many albums as Zeppelin and the Who, and, like those bands, they had done it without compromise and without suffering the internal personnel shake-ups that plagued other groups.

Throughout their first decade Black Sabbath kept the same line-up; Terry ('Geezer') Butler on bass, Bill Ward on drums, Tony Iommi on lead guitar and Ozzy Osbourne on vocals. Between them they created a distinctive sound, at times heavily oppressive yet always underpinned by an attractive melodic line, as on 'Iron Man', say. After *Sabbath, Bloody Sabbath*, however, the band underwent severe management troubles and did not record another album for some while. It was July 1975 when *Sabotage*, Sabbath's sixth album, appeared, and while there was still that definitive Sabbath sound on most of the tracks, ('Symptom Of The Universe' for instance) 'Supertzar', with its use of the English Chamber Choir, was a change in direction which Ozzy Osbourne, for one, didn't welcome. There were small signs that all was not well in the band. Even so, the band held together, and their seventh album, *Technical Ecstacy*, appeared in October 1976. Again there were elements foreign to the old Sabbath in the mix – an orchestral sound on the ballad 'She's Gone' – and even out-and-out rockers like 'Dirty Women' lacked the dark power of earlier classics like 'N.I.B.'. But the band were still as popular as ever, their albums consistently in the US charts, earning gold albums for sales, and things didn't come to a head until after the recording of *Never Say Die*, released in October 1978. The title track was the last thing Osbourne recorded with Sabbath (though his own solo live album, *Talk Of The Devil*, features four sides of classic Sabbath tracks!). He had left the band briefly in the winter of 1977/78, replaced temporarily by ex-Savoy Brown vocalist Dave Walker, but his return to the fold lasted only until early 1979 when he quit for good.

Osbourne's departure acted like a catalyst on the band; change was in the air. Ex-Rainbow vocalist Ronnie Dio joined the band – temporarily, at first, but later to stay – and in July Geezer Butler quit the band, being replaced by ex-Quartz bassist Geoff Nicols for a brief period before Butler returned in time to record their new album. This line-up recorded *Heaven And Hell*, released in April 1980, touring the US later in the year. Then, in November, Bill Ward left through ill health and Vinnie Appice took over on drums.

The new Anglo-American Black Sabbath released its first album, *Mob Rules* in October 1981, and, annoyed somewhat by the release of *Live At Last* (June 1980) which

featured Sabbath's original line-up, they put out their own live double album, *Live Evil*, in 1982, with Dio's distinctive vocal sound (which had changed the band's direction on the two studio albums) being heard on vinyl singing the older Sabbath anthems. The fans didn't seem to mind, and Sabbath sold at many albums as ever (by 1981 they had sold well over 8 million worldwide), but the honeymoon with the two Americans was relatively short-lived. In 1982 Ronnie Dio left the band, taking Vinnie Appice with him, to form his own band, Dio. Bill Ward returned to the band, while for a time Sabbath struggled on without a vocalist. Then, when it seemed that the band was at an end, they announced that their new vocalist was none other than ex-Deep Purple frontman Ian Gillan, whose own group, Gillan, had ceased the previous year. The band recorded its best album for years, *Born Again*, released in 1983, with ex-Electric Light Orchestra drummer, Bev Bevan coming in when Bill Ward again left through depleted health. *Born Again* was interesting in the way Sabbath adapted their style to accommodate Gillan's vocals while keeping their distinctive guitar-bass sound. It wasn't the old Sabbath, but it was just as good.

In March 1984 Ian Gillan quit the band and once again the search began for a new vocalist, Ron Keel (ex-Steeler) being the favourite amongst those rumoured for the job, though to date no replacement has been announced. But Bill Ward is back yet again and studio time has been booked in August 1984 to record the new Sabbath album, so any rumours of Sabbath's demise are premature. Sabbath will be here for years to come, their dark, heavy sound influencing a hundred lesser imitators.

Albums:

Black Sabbath (1970) *Paranoid* (1970) *Master Of Reality* (1971) *Black Sabbath Volume 4* (1972) *Sabbath, Bloody Sabbath* (1973) *Sabotage* (1975) *We Sold Our Soul For Rock 'n' Roll* (1975)* *Technical Ecstasy* (1976) *Greatest Hits* (1977)* *Never Say Die* (1978) *Live At Last* (1980) *Mob Rules* (1981) *Live Evil* (1982) *Born Again* (1983)

* Compilation albums.

Blue Oyster Cult

Strange, alien-looking symbols, airmens' uniforms, a curious reverence for the Canadian Mounted Police ('The Red And The Black') and an obsession with the fantastic – these are all elements of a band who have been called "The Thinking Man's Heavy Metal Animal". Thoughtful they are, and at times they can churn out heavy metal power-chords and thundering riffs with the best of them, but Blue Oyster Cult are too subtle and too changeable a beast to fit any convenient label. At times this changeability – their refusal to admit to labelling – has brought the critical comment that their music falls between two stools, being neither wholly Heavy Metal nor that of a wholly experimental/progressive group, but it's a comment that has no real validity. Blue Oyster Cult have always played a particular kind of mellow, highly technical and polished hard rock that sounds like no one else around. And if that failure to copy any style but their own has kept them from the *real* big time, then Eric Bloom and the band seen quite happy with that.

The Cult first came together in embryonic form in 1967, in Long Island, New York, when fledgling rock critics, R. Meltzer and Sandy Pearlman (later to become B.O.C.'s manager) got a band together. As Soft White Underbelly (a name they still use when playing incognito, as in the UK in 1981), they brought in their fellow Stony Brook university students, Albert Bouchard (drums), Donald "Buck Dharma" Roeser (lead guitar) and Alan Lanier (keyboards/rhythm guitar). They cut an album for Elektra under this name with Les Bronstein on vocals, but it remained unreleased. Meltzer had stepped into the background, remaining part of the band's writing team. Then, after further shake-ups in the vocal department, Eric Bloom joined as vocalist/guitarist in 1969, and when Joe Bouchard, Albert's brother, joined as bassist, the classic Blue Oyster Cult line-up was completed. They changed their name to Oaxaca, recording yet another unreleased album for Elektra, and toured the clubs and concert halls. Pearlman, certain of their eventual success, suggested the change of name and image. They adopted the ancient symbol of Cronos, the Titan God (it also means "Chaos") and won a recording contract with Columbia Records as Blue Oyster Cult in 1971. Within months their debut album, its material long prepared on the road, was out in America.

Called simply *Blue Oyster Cult*, their debut album is one of the most delightful first outings ever released. The purity of guitar tones, the first-rate musicianship and the melodic complexity of the songs won the band a cult (sic) following at once. 'Workshop Of The Telescopes' in particular was impressive, and gave a clear indication of what lay ahead for the band.

By touring as openers for Alice Cooper, Blue Oyster

19

Cult got to play in front of large audiences across the States for the first time, and their popularity increased greatly. *Tyranny And Mutation* appeared in 1973, including several good rockers – 'The Red And The Black' and 'Hot Rail To Hell' amongst them. But the Cult were no simple headbanging act; there were no high-pitched screaming vocals, and no thundering drums-bass riffs. What there was differed considerably from the expected Heavy norm:– tight three-part vocal harmonies, soft drum sounds and lyrical interludes. Nonetheless, no one could say that it wasn't a hard rock album, and with *Secret Treaties* in 1974 Blue Oyster Cult demonstrated that they were capable of much greater musical progress than most heavy bands. It was this album that lifted Blue Oyster Cult out of the small-band-with-cult-following bracket and into the big-nationwide league. It also illustrated the Cult's fascination with the fantastic, especially in the final two tracks, 'Flaming Telepaths' and 'Astronomy' (both of them longer, subtler tracks than anything the Cult had attempted before).

Eric Bloom, the band's spokesman, has said that B.O.C. (like the Scorpions!) like to end each phase of their development with a live album. 1975's double live treat, *On Your Feet Or On Your Knees*, was a splendid culmination of their first phase and remains, perhaps, their finest live showcase. The album which followed, in 1976, *Agents Of Fortune*, was a curious and different mix, for the main part much softer than pervious albums and in some respects rather patchy. Patti Smith's vocals on 'The Revenge Of Vera Gemini' (subdued but evident) were a minor bonus, but generally it was not the Cult at their best. With one exception. The single released from *Agents Of Fortune*, '(Don't Fear) The Reaper', is Blue Oyster Cult at their very best – a fact recognised by the record-buying public, who made the song a Top Twenty hit. It has since become one of the Cult's anthems, and in September 1976 was No. 12 in the US charts (staying in the top forty for 14 weeks, as well as becoming a hit worldwide). 'The Reaper' helped boost sales of the album and gave B.O.C. their first big hit as well. It also allowed them, to indulge in a lavish stage set for their live shows – $100,000 of lasers alone! – which they took with them worldwide.

Spectres, their 1977 album, is perhaps their most esoteric and mystical album and, together with their live album, *Some Enchanted Evening*, released in 1978, ended their second, far more experimental phase. Like many bands in the HM category, Blue Oyster Cult have not allowed commercial success to keep them from playing to their public, and 1978 saw a massive tour by the band, with almost 250 concerts in front of more than half a million people.

Mirrors appeared in 1979, a heavier album which won little critical applause, though the yet-heavier *Cultosaurus Erectus* in 1980 did win wide praise, with its much more assured sound; a powerful reassertion of their standing in the Heavy Metal league, especially on tracks like 'Lips In The Hills' (though 'Monsters' actually moved between heavy rock and jazz in a most disconcerting manner!). It also continued their dalliance with fantasy (Michael Moorcock, the fantasy and science fiction writer helped pen 'Black Blade').

1981's *Fire Of Unknown Origin*, was their most melodic outing and spawned a second top forty hit (just!) with 'Burnin' For You'. Again there was a collaboration with Moorcock, this time on 'Veteran Of The Psychic Wars', but the science fiction element was not allowed to overwhelm the musical content of the album. The importance of this alien imagery was made clear with their next live offering, *Extraterrestrial Live*, in 1982 – not merely in the album cover's imagery (which depicts an esoteric alien priest standing in the entrance-hatch of a massive UFO, while the band stand nearby, unconcerned, in fliers' uniforms) but in the choice of material. It is the lease impressive of their live albums, but it has its moments (listen to the guitar solo on 'Cities On Flame').

For a time it seemed possible that *Extraterrestrial Live* might be the last to be heard from the Cult. Donald Roeser had released a solo album, as Buck Dharma, in late '82, *Flat Out*, and Albert Bouchard had quit the band after the Castle Donington concert in 1981, to be replaced by drummer Rick Downey for the remaining commitments. But all rumours of their demise were scotched late in 1983 when *The Revolution By Night* appeared, backed up by a massive American tour. The album was their best for some time and Bouchard's contributions to the writing (he was their major songwriter before he left) were not missed as greatly as some feared. Fifteen years on they've still enough ideas to keep their music sounding fresh – and they can still rock hard enough to satisfy the heaviest of the heavies.

Albums:
Blue Oyster Cult (1971) *Tyranny and Mutation* (1973) *Secret Treaties* (1974) *On Your Feet Or On Your Knees* (1975) *Agents Of Fortune* (1976) *Spectres* (1977) *Some Enchanted Evening* (1978) *Mirrors* (1979) *Cultosaurus Erectus* (1980) *Fire Of Unknown Origin* (1981) *Extraterrestrial Live* (1982) *The Revolution By Night* (1983)

Deep Purple

Deep Purple have their origins back in 1967 when ex-Searcher ('Needles and Pins'!) Chris Curtis wanted to form a group called Roundabout. He was to be the vocalist, and recruited Jon Lord (organ) and Nick Simper (bass) from the Garden, the backing group to the legendary Flowerpot Men. Lord and Simper recommended 22-year-old guitarist Ritchie Blackmore, and he too joined the fledgling band. Then, when Curtis dropped out of the project, Rod Evans, vocalist with the Maze joined, bringing in with him the drummer from the Maze, Ian Paice. Deep Purple was born. It was March 1968, they had toured Scandinavia as Roundabout, discarded the name, cut their first album in an 18-hour stint and were about to tour America. 'Hush', a Joe South number, was released as a single. Fingers were crossed.

From the first Jon Lord had envisaged Deep Purple (almost called "Concrete God" – can you imagine *Concrete God In Rock*?!) as a British Vanilla Fudge, heavy but melodic, and their first few singles (and much of the material on their early albums) was in the Fudge mould, heavy covers of popular tunes (like The Beatles' 'Help'). 'Hush' surprised everyone by going to No. 4 in the US charts, and the follow-up single, 'Kentucky Woman' (a Neil Diamond number) went to No. 38 later in the year. Deep Purple were a success, yet in their own country they were ignored, being seen as just another pop group. This low profile in the UK is reflected in the fact that their second album, *The Book Of Taliesyn*, rush-released in October 1968 in the States, was not issued in Britain until July the next year. Yet all was not perfect on the other side of the Atlantic; their record company, Tetragrammaton, eventually went broke, owing the band a lot of money, and on the live circuit Purple were thrown off Cream's farewell tour of the States.

Live, the early Purple were aggressive and very loud, though not blues-based, like so many other groups of the time. But whereas they considered themselves a heavy, progressive band, the media played on their lightweight pop image. March 1969 saw the band in the studios recording their third album, *Deep Purple*, which, when it was released, had the poorest showing yet of any of their albums in the charts, failing to reach the top 60, as the others had done. The band's core (Lord, Blackmore and Paice) decided something had to be done, and, unknown to their management, they fired Simper and Evans and brought in Ian Gillan and Roger Glover respectively vocalist and bassist with the moderately successful Episode Six and recorded a single ('Hallelujah'). Six days after their last performance with Simper and Evans they made their first appearance with the new line-up at the Speakeasy Club, London on 10th July 1969. The "classic" Deep Purple were launched.

The transformation from an aggressive pop group to a heavy rock group was sudden and decisive in Purple's development. From the very first the new band were playing 'Speed King', 'Child In Time' and 'Into The Fire', tracks which, when they appeared on the classic *Deep Purple In Rock* album in June 1970, changed heavy rock and spawned a thousand imitators. But in the interim Purple were also involved in a wholly different project, Jon Lord's *Concerto For Group And Orchestra*, performed with the 100 musicians of The London Philharmonic at the Royal Albert Hall in London on September 24th, 1969. The concert and the album (the event was also televised in England) brought the band critical attention and, at long last, respectability. But it was the release of *Deep Purple In Rock* five months later that laid the foundations for Purple's success. It was unadulterated heavy rock; riff-based heavy metal that blistered the ears. But whilst it went to No. 4 in the UK charts it did nothing in the States. Deep Purple's popularity had curiously reversed itself. Their single 'Black Night' was No. 2 in the UK charts in May 1970, whilst 'Strange Kind Of Woman', released in February 1971, reached No. 8.

With the release of *Fireball* (July 1971 in the States, September in the UK) Deep Purple had their first No. 1 album in the UK (it was No. 32 in the States), although, curiously enough, the music was something of a disappointment after *In Rock*. But Purple's star was in the ascendant and *Machine Head*, released in the summer of 1972, was vintage Purple, with 'Highway Star', 'Smoke On The Water' and 'Space Truckin'' all becoming stage favourites. Not only was it No. 1 in the UK charts, but was also No. 7 in the US. It was their best-selling album, with over 3 million copies bought by die-hard Purple fans. 1972 saw the band undertake five major American tours, material from which can be found on the live *Made In Japan* album, released in the winter of 1972/3. On 'Highway Star' particularly the pure power of the band at this time can be felt physically. Yet at the moment of their greatest success, the band was already disintegrating.

The strains were showing already on the 1972 tours where there was a constant battle of egos concerning the length of solos, but these tensions came to the surface during the recording of the ironically titled *Who Do We Think We Are* between July and October 1972. Uninspired and lacking in the raw energy for which the band was justly famous, the album was a grave mistake (even while it went to No. 4 in the UK charts) and precipitated the demise of that classic Purple line-up. Only 'Woman From Tokyo' saved the album from being an utter dodo. From this time on Blackmore and Gillan were no longer

talking, and Gillan was making his way separately to concerts. Added to this strain was the fact that Roger Glover was slowly being eased out of the band; in June 1973 he resigned, following the last concert of the classic Purple line-up in Osaka in June 29th.

Ex-Trapeze bassist Glenn Hughes was drafted in to replace Glover, and the band started looking for a new vocalist. Blackmore wanted ex-Free frontman Paul Rodgers, but Rodgers turned the job down, and so, unexpectedly and anonymously, Purple advertised for a new vocalist in the pages of Britain's rock paper, *Melody Maker*. Through this means David Coverdale joined the band in July 1973. The honeymoon period for the new group was brief. *Burn* was recorded in November that year under good conditions and, released in February 1974, went to No. 3 in the UK charts and No. 9 in the States. In terms of popularity the new group was bigger than the previous line-up, and their 1974 US tour climaxed with a concert at Ontario Motor Speedway in California, where an estimated 300,000 fans saw Purple headline an all-day concert. But there was unhealthy competition between Hughes and Coverdale for vocal spots, and Blackmore was beginning to lose interest in what the band was doing.

Stormbringer, released in November 1974, saw the band heading into a new area, with more blues and soul influences entering the music via Coverdale (who shares credits for writing all the tracks on the album). Blackmore was taking a back seat, and his own ideas were being held back for a solo project in early 1975 which was to become, eventually, the first Rainbow album. The split which was to result in Whitesnake and Rainbow began during the recording of *Stormbringer*, which proved the least commercially successful of Purple's 70s albums.

Blackmore's last concert with Purple was at the Paris Olympia on April 7th 1975. It seemed Deep Purple was dead, and Jon Lord and Ian Paice wanted to call it a day, but Coverdale and Hughes pressed them to recruit a new guitarist, and Tommy Bolin was brought into the band.

From the first it proved a mistake. Bolin was a drug addict, brilliant when on form but sometimes unable even to play guitar, let alone play it well. *Come Taste The Band* resulted from the new line-up and got to No. 19 in the UK charts in December 1975, a poor showing by Purple's standards (it only reached No. 43 in the States!) The magic had fled, the album was insipid at best, and disaster dogged the band on their big Far East tour. Finally, on March 15th, 1976, Deep Purple played their last concert at the Liverpool Empire Theatre, David Coverdale quitting five minutes after coming off stage. Nine months later Bolin was dead of heroin addiction.

The statistics alone remained – along with the albums – to tell the story:– 20 million albums sold in 13 years and nearly £10 million in record royalties. Rumours abounded about the classic line-up reforming, only to be abundantly scotched. But then in May 1984 came the surprising announcement that the 1970–73 line-up were back together again, planning a tour and getting ideas together for an album:– Blackmore, Paice, Glover, Lord and Gillan – considered by many to be *the* Deep Purple.

AC/DC watch out – the heaviest of the heavies are back!

Albums:
Shades Of Deep Purple (1968) *The Book Of Taliesyn* (1969) *Deep Purple* (1969) *Concerto For Group And Orchestra* (1970) *Deep Purple In Rock* (1970) *Fireball* (1971) *Machine Head* (1972) *Made In Japan* (1972) *Who Do We Think We Are* (1973) *Burn* (1974) *Stormbringer* (1974) *Come Taste The Band* (1975) *Made In Europe* (1976) *Last Concert In Japan* (1977) *Powerhouse* (1977) *In Concert 1970–72* (1980)

Compilations:
The Best Of Deep Purple (US, 1972) *Purple Passages* (US, 1972) *24 Carat Purple* (UK, 1975) *The Deep Purple Singles A's and B's* (UK, 1978) *When We Rock We Rock And When We Roll We Roll* (US, 1978)

Def Leppard

With its industrial landscape of steel mills and grey coal pits, Sheffield, England, might appear to be a natural breeding ground for heavy metal music. However, its melodic sons have usually followed the lure of the synthesiser: Human League (Joe Elliot, DL's frontman once lived one hundred yards from Phil Oakey), Heaven 17, the Comsat Angels, Gang of Four, etc etc. Def Leppard are the dynamic exception.

The band was formed in 1977 when Joe Elliot, a 19-year-old van driver, Rick Allen, a 15-year-old schoolboy and drummer, and guitar player Pete Willis met up with Rick Savage, 18 and working for British Rail, who supplied the necessary bass line. The bright young men called their group Atomic Mass and soon garnered a faithful following in Sheffield pubs and clubs like the Woodsborough Dale Miners Welfare Club, Crook's Working Man's Club and the High Green Liberal Club. Joined by Steven Clark on second guitar, who (with Elliot) began writing original material to vary a set until then made up of cover versions.

It was still the heyday of punk in England and their hard rock style was unfashionable. As Joe puts it, "Punk rock was heavy metal with singers who couldn't sing and guitar players who couldn't solo." Adds Rik Savage "Though we're not really *influenced* by punk, we *did* cut 10 minute guitar solos." This no-frills approach, characteristic of the British New Wave of Heavy Metal, soon garnered attention, particularly when after changing the band's name to Def Leppard (a Joe Elliot idea), they saved enough money to record a three-track EP in a Hull studio. *Getcha Rocks Off* was released on Def Leppard's own Bludgeon Riffola label. Praised by press and disc jockeys alike, the band was soon signed by Phonogram and taken under the wing of canny, Jewish New York manager Peter Mensch, fresh from his success with AC/DC.

Their first album *On Through the Night* came out in 1980 and the band embarked on their first American tour in May of the same year. It was already a far cry from their first gig at Westfield School, Sheffield, for which they were paid five pounds! The album was a hit in the US, just falling short of the Top Fifty. But American kids took to the boys in Def Leppard in a big way; here was a heavy metal group with verve and personality and without the faceless aspects and beer bellies of most homegrown bands in the field of metaldom.

For their second album *High 'n' Dry*, they were paired with Foreigner and AC/DC producer Robert 'Mutt' Lange and the combination worked wonders. Mutt added much in the way of dynamics to the band's sound after a gruelling and lengthy recording time. In July 1981, Pete Willis left the band and Phil Collen from Girl replaced him. "When Pete left, we were like, overnight, down to one guitarist.

That put Steve under a lot of pressure. He'd have to do 10 more solos – which he could *do*, but I don't really think he wanted to. We're a definite two guitar band," recalls Elliot.

High 'n' Dry reached the Top Forty on both sides of the Atlantic and the band supported it with a gruelling bout of touring, mostly in America, where their audience just kept on growing as they switched from opening for AC/DC and Rainbow to headlining major venues in their own right. The Mutt Lange big mix of melody and muscle pushed the album's US sales beyond the two million mark and the band and he teamed up again for their third album *Pyromania*.

Recorded at great expense and in 10 studios (although only two are credited on the sleeve), *Pyromania* is a major step forward, *using* Joe's voice, as the fifth instrument of the band. The album spawned several hits including 'Photograph' (about Marilyn Monroe, although it doesn't mention her name) and 'Rock Of Ages', the video of which proved a massive hit with MTV viewers. The mega-tour that followed saw Def Leppard playing to over one million Americans, selling over 7 million albums and reaching number 2 (behind Michael Jackson's *Thriller*) in the US charts, while 'Photograph' reached the top 20.

Touring is a way of life for Def Leppard, a life they enjoy as the travelling entourage is a close-knit family affair: tour manager Robert Allen is drummer Richard's brother and doubles as sound engineer. The enthusiasm they conjure up in performance is electrifying, with singer Joe Elliot trying throughout to make the audience clap and them complaining they didn't clap *loud* enough. Joe's customary stage outfit is a Union Jack strip, sometimes hiding a stars and stripes underlayer revealed in the later stages of the performance. A smouldering set of superbly crafted rock songs, highlighting the hit singles and an old favourite from *High 'n' Dry*, 'Bringing On The Heartbreak', is performed at breakneck speed, usually ending up with the familiar old Creedence Clearwater Revival number 'Travelling Man', a rip-roaring rocker with two neat guitar breaks and a sheet of flames ending.

As *Rolling Stone* pointed out at a Def Leppard concert: "Every other kid was playing air guitar perfectly in sync with the real instruments onstage – a sign that indicates a band is truly hip among heavy-metal fans." Def Leppard are certainly that, and we'll certainly hear and see much more of their electrifying blues riffs as they enter the studio with wizard Mutt Lange again in the summer of 1984, keeping the fans happy with the release of a new version of *High 'n' Dry*, with a remixed version of 'Bringing On The Heartbreak' and the previously unreleased rocker 'Me And My Wine'.

Def Leppard: the young naturals of heavy metal.

Albums:

On Through the Night (1980) *High 'n' Dry* (1981) *Pyromania* (1983) *High 'n' Dry (mark II)* (1984)

Dio

Back in 1957 Ronald Padavona, a native of Portsmouth, New Hampshire, was living in New York and playing in a school band called The Vegas Kings. Padavona had studied classical trumpet as a child, but had switched to electric bass. Around this time he changed his name to Ronnie Dio and became the group's vocalist, as well as bassist. The Vegas Kings became Ronnie & The Red Caps, who in turn became Ronnie Dio and The Prophets, who, between 1961 and 1967, cut seven singles.

The Autumn of 1967 saw Ronnie Dio and his guitarist Nick Pantas leave the Prophets behind them and form The Electric Elves (subsequently The Elves). The group had little luck, changing record companies several times and cutting only two more singles. Then, in the summer of 1970, the band was involved in a car crash, in which guitarist Pantas was killed and keyboards man Doug Thaler was hospitalised. The group decided to carry on, as Elf, bringing in Mickey Lee Soule on keyboards and guitar to join Garry Driscoll on drums and Dave Feinstein on guitar. When Thaler came back it was as a guitarist. This group cut *Elf* for Epic in 1972, produced by Deep Purple's Roger Glover, then toured the States twice as Purple's support band in late '72.

After a shake-up in early 1973 (Feinstein and Thaler were out, bassist Craig Gruber in, with Dio concentrating on vocals and lyrics) Elf went to England to cut a further two albums for Purple Records, *Carolina County Ball*, in 1974 and *Trying To Burn The Sun* in 1975. It was this four-piece Elf that Ritchie Blackmore adopted as his first Rainbow group in May 1975, recording *Ritchie Blackmore's Rainbow*. Yet by September only Ronnie Dio remained in Rainbow, after one of Blackmore's periodic purges.

Between September 1975 and late '78 Blackmore, Dio and Cozy Powell were to form the core of a fluctuating Rainbow, and Blackmore and Dio were to jointly pen most of the material for three albums:- the debut, *Rainbow Rising* in 1976, and *Long Live Rock 'n' Roll* in 1978. The melodic strengths Ronnie Dio had shown on Elf's third album, *Try To Burn The Sun*, were given a sharper edge in Rainbow by Blackmore's desire to create a much heavier rock feel than Deep Purple had shown in his last few years with them. Songs like 'Catch The Rainbow', 'Tarot Woman' and 'Long Live Rock 'n' Roll' were the result of their collaboration.

Ozzy Osbourne's departure from Black Sabbath in 1979 left a gap in the band's line-up that seemed unfillable. The group had been preparing for a big American tour in September, and called in Ronnie Dio as a temporary stop-gap. Dio had left Rainbow in January 1979 (of his own choice, apparently), and late in '79 he became a full-time member of Sabbath. Dio's voice, markedly different from Ozzy's, forced a change in Black Sabbath's musical direction, especially on tracks like 'Children Of The Sea', on the *Heaven And Hell* album, his first studio outing with the band in April 1980. Dio's experience in Rainbow shaped all he did in the next three years with Sabbath. *Mob Rules*, his second album with Sabbath, saw him playing with Vinnie Appice, who had been recruited in place of the departed Bill Ward. Once again Dio shared writing credits with Tony Iommi, and once again his influence is writ large on the resultant material.

Ronnie Dio cut one other album with Black Sabbath before he finally left them in 1982 to carry out the solo project he had abandoned to join them in 1979, and that was the live double album, *Live At Last*, where he carried off the difficult task of singing the old Sabbath anthems to the masses who had adulated Ozzy. To his credit Ronnie Dio managed to re-vitalise Black Sabbath during his stay with them (as Ian Gillan was to do in his brief stay in 1983). But then he moved on, taking drummer Vinnie Appice with him, to form Dio, the band.

Ronnie Dio had a clear idea of who he wanted as bassist for his new group and brought in Jimmy Bain, who had played with him in Rainbow in the mid Seventies. Between leaving Rainbow in August 1978 and joining Ronnie Dio, Bain had spent three years in Wild Horses, alongside ex-Thin Lizzy guitarist Brian Robertson, and had then played on and off with various people, including a tour with Thin Lizzy. When Dio and Appice quit Sabbath he just happened to be available and joined at once.

Which left the problem of getting the right guitarist. Jimmy Bain came up with the solution; whilst touring with Lizzy he had been impressed by the lead guitarist of their support act, Sweet Savage, a 21-year-old Belfast boy named Vivian Campbell. Ronnie Dio brought him to London for an audition and was impressed enough to ask him to join the band at once. Dio were complete.

The first album, recorded in Los Angeles, Ronnie Dio's home base, was a slight change from the material Dio had been writing with Rainbow and Sabbath. For the first time it could be uncompromising. The result was the hard rocking but highly melodic *Holy Diver*, released in February 1983. It found an audience already appreciative of Ronnie Dio's work with Rainbow and Sabbath and went to No. 13 in the UK charts in June 1983, whilst selling respectably in the States (Warners initially pressed 40,000 – it sold 500,000). And, of course, Dio took their show on the road, their stage-set using Medieval imagery mixed with the modern technology of lasers to create a visually impressive spectacle. With Vinnie Appice raised up high above the band and Ronnie Dio forcefully delivering the

goods up front, they're a sight not to be missed. And for Ronnie Dio's Rainbow and Sabbath fans, there are always a few of the old numbers thrown in during the live set – 'Heaven and Hell, 'Man On The Silver Mountain' and 'Stargazer' amongst them.

The summer of 1984 should see Dio's second album, *The Last In Line*, out in the shops, with a single from it, 'Mystery', scheduled for their US single. Once again it's a showcase of the clarity, power and melody the band possesses in abundance.

Albums:

Holy Diver (1983)   *The Last In Line* (1984)

Dokken

The Scorpions respect them, Def Leppard chose them to open several of their concerts in the USA in Spring 1983, the German heavy metal community adore them, and the rest of the L.A. hard rock community will tell you that they're the best band to come out of the city of the fallen angels in many a year. Yet at present their reputation rests on one album (twice recorded) and – particularly in the UK, where they haven't even a recording deal – on word-of-mouth reportage.

Dokken, that peculiarly German-sounding band, have never really promoted themselves in the way that their glam-rock L.A. contemporaries seem to. There's something a bit more serious about their music, and, if a comparison needs to be drawn, it's perhaps to the early days of Black Sabbath and Deep Purple when those bands were considered "Underground". Dokken's music contains elements of those two seminal bands, particularly on tracks like 'Breaking The Chains', the title cut from their 1983 album, *Breaking The Chains*.

For those Heavy Metal fans with an eagle eye and a copy of a 1981 Don Dokken album called *Breakin' The Chains* in their collection, no, you're not mistaken or hallucinating, it's just that Don Dokken, lead vocalist, guitarist, songwriter and band leader of Dokken, first put the album together as a solo project and then, when he'd found the right musicians, re-recorded it with his new group. The result (if you haven't got it) is a Heavy Metal classic to rival the best of Rainbow, Purple and Kiss – certainly one of the finest heavy albums of 1983.

Dokken are a raunchy, guitar-driven rock band who have blended the new wave Metal sound with an old hard-rocking style with first-rate songs and excellent vocal harmonies. George Lynch's lead guitar playing (listen to the live 'Paris Is Burning') is another element that reminds you – at first listening anyway – of Ritchie Blackmore at his best, though there's nothing plagiaristic about his style. Behind him is one of the most powerful rhythm sections not owned by AC/DC, with Juan Croucier on bass (and backing vocals) and Mick Brown on drums.

1985 should see a second Dokken album out – it's presently being recorded (once again in West Germany,

the band's semi-adopted home) and meanwhile Don Dokken has been providing the vocals and lyrics for Scorpion drummer Hermann Harebell's solo album. So, if you missed the first, then catch the second: you won't, I'm sure, be disappointed.

Albums:
Breakin' The Chains (1981, Don Dokken)   *Breaking The Chains* (1983, Dokken)

Euro-Metal

Back in the late sixties it seemed to most British and American observers that Mainland Europe was a desert as far as good rock music was concerned. They sent us Bert Kampfert, we sent them back Petula Clark and Tony Bennett. But it wasn't so. Not really. Because out there in Mainland Europe (both sides of the curtain, though let's concentrate on the West for now) was a whole budding generation of rock musicians who were buying import copies of Zeppelin, Sabbath, Purple and Co. by the wheelbarrow-full. Europe had seemed the last true home of the fanatical jazz fan, yet millions of kids were growing up wanting to be like Jimmy Page, Ozzy Osbourne, Roger Glover . . .

My first encounter with Mainland Europe's answer to Western Rock dates from 1970 and the discovery of two German bands, Amon Duul II and Can. In time the Duul grew dull and Can became – jazzers. But at the start they were heavy. *Very* heavy. And not a brass band in sight. Amon Duul II brought out *Yeti* (which featured Dave Anderson on bass – later drafted into Hawkwind, before Lemmy took over) and on tracks like 'Soap Shop Rock' blasted any ideas I had that the Germans couldn't rock.

Tago Mago by Can arrived a little while later that year and was loud enough – with Holger Czukay's bass-playing dominant – to dislodge books from shelves and pictures from walls. But then that whole scene seemed to die – grew introspective and too experimental (though Duul did produce *Dance Of The Lemmings*, the best space-rock album that Hendrix never made). But even then the Scorpions were forming and the Schenker brothers were about to begin their slow climb to eventual super-stardom . . . and it wasn't just in Germany that things were beginning to happen. All over Western (and Northern) Europe bands were forming, playing Heavy Metal . . . and in the late seventies they began to emerge.

This doesn't aim to be a history however, simply a round up of the top (currently) second league bands in the European Heavy Metal scene. A brief alphabetical introduction, if you like, indicating where some of the more interesting HM sounds hail from.

ACCEPT are from Solingen in West Germany and were, for a time, tipped to eventually be as big as Sabbath. They're an excellent two-guitar five-piece with five albums to their credit. Epic signed them in late '83 and they've

come from the same stable as The Scorpions. Their power and melodic flair could well lift them into the top league if they can get exposure in the States. *Balls To The Wall*, their 1983 album, is a good introduction, though by no means their best album.

ACID are a Belgian band, coming from Brugges. Another five-piece, they're a 'Black Metal' (horror rock) band with a female vocalist, Kate. Their hammer-and-chisel attack can be experienced on *Acid*, released on their own Giant label in 1983. They're not another **VENOM** though – much more into motor bikes, sex and drink than true devilry!

BULLET are another West German band in the Scorpions stable (with manager Dieter Dierks controlling them). They've two albums out, *Execution* and *No Mercy* (1984), which show this four-piece, two guitar band (all German bands seem to sport duelling flying-V guitarists a-la-Scorpions!) to be a second division AC/DC. Which isn't a bad thing to be!

EASY ACTION, Sweden's latest export (at least, to the UK market) seem to be Hanoi Rocks copyists. Formed in 1983, their *Easy Action* debut, released in 1984 is a curious glitter-Metal platter. Sound and image are good, but they seem lacking a touch on originality.

Another Swedish band, this time with a Journey-like sound, are the **EF BAND**. They've been going since 1978 with various line-ups and have recorded three albums to date. Their following, whilst still small, is fanatical.

ELOY are rather an enigma, because they're on a heavy metal label in the UK and yet strictly they're a symphonic pomp rock band with heavy undertones. They brought out ten albums in the seventies and early eighties before getting a British deal and anyone who enjoys science fiction epics will love their work. They've recently become a five-piece after being a four-piece for so long. German, they're the brainchild of guitarist/vocalist Frank Bornemann, and play some of the classiest music that you've never heard on the radio.

EUROPE are a relatively new Swedish band whose *Wings Of Tomorrow* album (1984) shows them to possess considerable skill and class. They're rather like MSG in their approach and, with their four-man line-up, could well break out from their home market and make a big impact on America and the UK.

If you want an excellent mainstream Heavy Metal band who play slaughterhouse rock for brain-damaged rape-and-pillage victims (music for the modern barbarian) then try Swedish 4-piece **HEAVY LOAD**, Heavy Metal's Vikings. Formed in 1977, they've produced four good albums so far, their music being in the Iron Maiden run-for-the-hills mould.

HIGHWAY CHILE are from Holland and have two albums, *Storybook Heroes* (1983) and *Rock & Roll Blitzkrieg* (1984), on offer. The title of the second gives an indication of their straightforward approach to the HM field.

MERCYFUL FATE are a woefully-neglected Danish band whose high-energy, Judas Priest-style music might eventually win them great rewards. They're a five-piece from Kopenhagen, fronted by the colourful King Diamond. Two albums, *Corpse Without A Soul* (1982) and *Melissa* (1983) are well worth checking out.

PICTURE are from Hilversum, Holland, a five-piece power-chord band who formed in Autumn 1979. Their *Diamond Dreamer* album (also released as *Nighthunter*) did well on the Heavy Metal charts in the UK. They've got four albums out, and whilst they seem fated to remain a second division band, they do produce a particularly pure HM sound.

ELECTRIC SUN (no, it's not out of order!) is the band put together by Uli Jon **ROTH**, the former Scorpions guitarist, whose compositions with Michael Schenker on early Scorpions albums gave the band its softer, more melodic side. *Firewind*, by his new three-piece band, pushes that side of his writing a bit further on. He's one of Europe's more thoughtful Metal-men.

TELEPHONE are massive in their homeland of France where the *Dure Limité* album went gold (400,000-plus copies sold). A five-piece sophisticated Heavy Metal band they make few concessions to the English language (though a poorly Anglicised version of *Dure Limité* does exist) but do have a small, fanatical UK following. They've been going six years now and are more popular in France than the better-known (in the UK) band Trust.

TNT are a four-piece Norwegian band who openly admit that they're Saxon addicts. Their music pays tribute to their heroes and by the end of this summer they should have their second album, *Knights Of The New Thunder* out in the shops.

TRANCE are another German two-flying-V-guitars band who produce a highly polished and greatly enjoyable sound which seems heavily influenced by the Scorpions. *Break Out* (1982) was their debut, followed up by *Power Infusion* in 1983. A third album is being recorded. They're derivative, it's true, but that doesn't stop them from being a very good, solid HM band.

Yet another Swedish HM band is **TRASH** whose *Watch out* album, released in 1983 demonstrates a highly original approach (something not often achieved by European Metal bands). They're a highly professional and skilful outfit too and don't, fortunately, live up to their name. Quite the contrary, they're probably the best of the new Swedish bands.

TRUST are a French band whose drummer, Nico McBrain recently joined Iron Maiden. *Trust,* their 1983 album for Epic, was their fourth since they formed in 1977. They're a five-piece, two guitar band and are famous for opening AC/DC's act on the latter's 1978 European tour. Like Telephone, they function best when singing in their native tongue, and produce some good hard-riffing metal.

Another Dutch band are **VANDENBERG** who look set to become as famous as their countrymen Golden Earring. They by-passed the usual round of signing to a Dutch company and then trying to sell overseas (a rigmarole which stopped Golden Earring from getting on at first) by going direct to Atlantic records in the UK. Two albums, *Vandenberg* (1982) and *Heading For A Storm* (1983) showcase this four-piece's quality. They've had big exposure, first in the UK in 1982 by touring with Michael Schenker, and then, more recently, in the States where they opened for Kiss on their nationwide tour. Their sound is developing. Incidentally, guitarist and frontman Adrian Vandenberg almost joined Whitesnake as lead guitarist when Micky Moody left. Enough said . . .

Last on this mini-guide to Euro-Metal is the German five-piece **WARLOCK**, whose female vocalist Dorothee Pesch gives them a slightly different sound. Two guitarists (of course) but a much more simple Heavy Metal sound than usually delivered by the German bands. Good competent headbanger music.

Euro-Metal is still developing, and with the Scorpions and Golden Earring (not to mention Michael Schenker!) finally making a big impact on the States, it may well be that the next big group will come from Europe. Having been imitators for so long they could easily become the next generation of innovators.

Lita Ford

Lita Ford was born in London in 1959. Both facts are surprising in the sense that as a veteran of the Runaways, one might expect a rather older, rather more American lady than the beautiful looking Ms. Ford. Lita Ford joined the Runaways in 1975 as their lead guitarist, alongside Joan Jett, Sandy West, Cherie Curry and Jackie Fox. They were the first all-female heavy rock band, formed by Kim Fowley, whose manipulation and hype launched the band big in the States and Japan. In their image they were years ahead of their time – schizophrenic sexual teases, school-girls whose pre-punk look, much influenced by Alice Cooper, captured the adolescent imagination in just the way it was supposed to. They made four albums (with various line-ups). *The Runaways*, 1976, *Queens Of Noise*, 1977, *Waitin' For The Night*, 1977, and *And Now The Runaways!* (aka, *Little Lost Girls*), 1979. These school-girls-out-for-sex-and-fun earned three gold records in Japan, but in 1978 Joan Jett quit the band because she felt the last album was *too* heavy, and the group folded. In their time they had spawned dozens of rumours of overdoses, fights and drunken orgies (some of it true, by all accounts) but for one member of the group the music had always been the thing. She was the heavy one in the Runaways, the one who gave them their power – especially on that final album. She was Lita Ford.

It's hard to accustom oneself to a mundane lifestyle after the heady heights of a rock'n'roll band, and Lita Ford's years as a make-up artist and assistant in a health spa following the folding of the Runaways were bad ones for her. She got bored easily and worked on material for a solo album, making demos. Phonogram heard them, loved them, and . . . brought her back into the heavy rock fold. Of course, she'd been involved in rock since she was eleven, had been a professional musician since her fifteenth year. Her first solo album, *Out For Blood*, released in 1983, was a disappointment, though. She had the wrong musicians, perhaps even the wrong attitude. The songs were weak and the resultant record bombed. Her tour with Rainbow didn't fare much better in the critics' eyes, though a spell supporting Black Sabbath won her a small following for her solo efforts. She began writing new material, brought together the musicians she wanted, and tried again.

The result of Lita Ford's reassessment is a stunning new album, *Dancin' On The Edge*, which shows Lita to be a

degree or so heavier than fellow female rockers Pat Benatar and Joan Jett. It's a hyper-charged album, with raw-edged fast rockers like 'Lady Killer' and 'Fire In My Heart' allowing Lita Ford to demonstrate that she's one of the best guitarists about, male or female. Drummer Randy Castillo, bassist Gordon Copley and rhythm guitarist Bobby Donati are now her regular back-up band, whilst Lita is singer, lead guitarist and sole composer. It's a combination that works well. It's also the first step on Lita Ford's post-Runaway progress towards international recognition.

Albums:

Out For Blood (1983)   *Dancin' On The Edge* (1984)

Golden Earring

1974 was a good year for Golden Earring. After thirteen years as a band, nine of those as top ten headliners in their home country of Holland, Golden Earring's single, 'Radar Love' was No. 13 in the US charts, and the album from which it was taken, *Moontan* was in the top twenty album charts, eventually going gold in the States. It seemed that they had broken into the big league of heavy acts at last, yet in the years that followed there was no repeat of that success and Golden Earring became, in the eyes of many, just another support band on the heavy rock/heavy metal circuit. Until 1982, that was, and the success of the single 'Twilight Zone' which climbed into the US top ten.

Bassist Rinus Gerritsen and lead guitarist George Kooymans first formed the band, then called the Golden Earrings, in 1961 (they were just fifteen!) and had a top ten hit with their first single, 'Please Go' in Holland in 1965. An album, *Just Earrings*, the first of nineteen to date, followed shortly afterwards. The band at that time was completed by Peter de Ronde on rhythm guitar, Jaap Eggermont on drums and Frans Krassenburg on vocals. In 1966 de Ronde and Krassenburg left and were replaced by Barry Hay, who remains the band's vocalist and rhythm guitarist to this day.

Heavily influenced by the British and US music scenes, Golden Earring (the name change had taken place by now) had their first tour of the States in 1969 and, with the release of the album *Eight Miles High* that year began to build a following outside their homeland. It was at this point that Jaap Eggermont left and Cesar Zuiderwijk joined the band on drums, completing the quartet that has stayed together since. Robert-Jan Stips was briefly in the band (1974–76) on keyboards, and Eelco Gelling on rhythm guitar in 1976/77, but otherwise the four-piece has maintained its stability.

The brand of driving hard rock, melodic but fast-paced, the band played – typified by 'Radar Love' – proved attractive to live audiences. The Who chose them as support band for their 1972 European tour, recognising

PHOTO: L.F.I./PAUL COX

this strength. Yet in the studio Golden Earring's music was often uninspired, their production indifferent, if not poor. Even so, they could come up with occasional classics, like the *Moontan* album, and the single 'Bombay' in 1976. A live album, released in 1977, is a better showcase of their material than the studio albums (which, until 1982, they produced themselves), yet even *Live* was something of a disappointment after the heights of 1974. Not until 1982 and the album *Cut*, produced by Shell Schellekens, did the good days return for the band. Videos of 'Twilight Zone' and their 1984 single, 'When The Lady Smiles' have won them an even bigger audience in the States. So, after two decades as a hard rock band, the Earring are once more on the road, touring the States on an extensive schedule, playing their hard, heavy, driving sound to a new generation of fans.

Albums:

Just Earrings (1965) *Winter Harvest* (1967) *Miracle Mirror* (1968) *On The Double* (1969) *Eight Miles High* (1969) *Golden Earring* (1970) *Seven Tears* (1971) *Together* (1972) *Moontan* (1973) *Switch* (1974) *To The Hilt* (1975) *Contraband* (1976) *Live* (1977) *Grab It For A Second* (1978) *No Promises, No Debts* (1979) *Prisoner Of The Night* (1980) *2nd Live* (1981) *Cut* (1982) *N.E.W.S.* (1984)

Sammy Hagar

Sammy Hagar was born in Monterey, California, in 1949 and grew up in Fontana. His father was a boxing champion and Hagar's earliest intention was to follow in his father's footsteps. Seeing Presley apparently changed his mind, and by the time he was 19, Sammy Hagar was in a small semi-pro band, the Justice Brothers, who played the club and bar circuit around San Bernadino in Southern California. It was a depressing time musically, a long, seven year stint with only marginal reward. Hagar never quite fitted with the musicians about him and when, in 1973, Ronnie Montrose invited him to join his new band, Montrose, Hagar accepted without a moment's hesitation.

Hagar was the front man Montrose had been seeking for some time, yet despite recording some great music on *Montrose* (1973) and *Paper Money* (1974), Hagar and Montrose didn't see eye to eye (the recriminations are still going on!) and Hagar left to pursue a solo career.

Hagar's first solo outing was *Nine On A Ten Scale*, released in 1976. It did moderately well, and Hagar took a band on the road to play his music live, the longest-running line-up including three of his former colleagues in Montrose:– bassist Bill Church, drummer Dennis Carmisi and keyboard player Alan Fitzgerald. With variations of this line-up he recorded four albums in the space of twenty months, *Sammy Hagar* in January 1977 (also known as *The Red Album!*), *Musical Chairs*, *All Night Long*, and the powerful live album, *Loud And Clear*, with its classic version of Hagar's stage favourite, 'Bad Motor Scooter'.

Whilst none of Hagar's early solo albums made the upper reaches of the charts, each sold respectably – in the 150,000–200,000 range – and won Hagar a solid following of fans. Live, he found himself supporting many of the big-name heavy bands on the US circuit, Kiss, Boston and Kansas amongst them, and occasionally touring on his own behalf.

1979 saw the release of *Street Machine* and *Danger Zone*, the first a classic, the second rather patchy but with moments, as on 'In The Night' where Hagar's strengths as songwriter and guitarist really showed themselves. By this time he had recruited guitarist Gary Pihl and keyboards man Geoff Workman, with Chuck Ruff on drums, but the band was to continue to fluctuate throughout the early 80s, when Hagar's record output temporarily diminished.

In 1982 *Standing Hampton* appeared, his first studio album in some time, and he had a small hit with the single 'I'll Fall In Love Again', which just touched the top forty in the States. But then, in 1983, Hagar really did break through into the commercial market with *Three Lock Box* (which spent eleven weeks in the top 20 from February to

April) and the single, 'Your Love Is Driving Me Crazy', which got to No. 13 in the US singles charts. The financial security this success gave to Hagar allowed him to launch a pet project in late '83, taking his friend, Journey guitarist Neal Schon, together with bassist Kenny Aaronson and drummer Mike Shrieve, on an 8-date tour of the San Francisco area to record a live album of all new material written by Schon and Hagar. It appeared, heavily over-dubbed, in 1984 as *Through The Fire* by HSAS. Hagar, meanwhile, had returned to the studios to record his new solo album, *Voice Of America*.

Whilst Sammy Hagar has never had the success outside the States that he's earned within, he has a respectable following worldwide and, with his subtler, more commercial music, is slowly extending his popularity.

Albums:

Nine On A Ten Scale (1976) *Sammy Hagar* (1977) *Musical Chairs* (1978) *All Night Long* (1978) *Loud And Clear* (1978) *Street Machine* (1979) *Danger Zone* (1979) *Live 1980* (1980) *Best Of* (1981)* *Standing Hampton* (1982) *The Very Best Of* (Red Alert – Dial Nine) (1982)* *Three Lock Box* (1983) *Through The Fire* (1984, HSAS) *Voice Of America* (1984)

* Compilation albums.

Hanoi Rocks

Tooting in South London is a strange place to find a group of Finnish punks whose sole aim is to conquer the rock'n' roll world with their own high-energy brand of gut rock, but so it goes. In late '82 you could find Hanoi Rocks, veterans of three albums, living in a dingy house in semi-suburbia, still awaiting the big break. Not that anyone who had heard those three albums, available only on import from the Swedish Johanna label, would have doubted that it was extremely likely that Hanoi Rocks would succeed. After all, one of their tracks, 'Love's An Injection' had been top of the Scandinavian charts for 2 weeks. . . .

Bangkok Shocks, Saigon Shakes launched Hanoi Rocks on an unsuspecting Scandinavian audience in 1981, an above-average debut with several more-than-interesting cuts, 'First Timer' and 'Tragedy' amongst them. Even then the emphasis on sex and drugs and rock'n'roll was heavy in the lyrics – not surprising in a band that cites Alice Cooper, the MC5 and the New York Dolls amongst its influences. At the time Rocks consisted of Gyp Casino (drums), Sam Yaffa (bass), Nasty Suicide (guitar/backing vocals), Andy McCoy (lead guitar/backing vocals) and Mike Monroe (lead vocals, saxophone, piano and harmonica). McCoy was the group's writer, while Monroe, blonde-haired and beautiful, gave the band their distinctive image, providing a focal point for the fans. *Oriental Beat* was the band's second album, released in 1982, and by then Hanoi Rocks had moved themselves to Tooting, shed drummer Casino and picked up British stick-man Razzle.

Imports of their first few albums and appearances at English rock clubs gave Hanoi Rocks their first exposure outside Scandinavia. Even so they were still considered by most to be just another hard rock band with aspirations and

PHOTO: C.B.S./TERRY LOTT

a sloppy attitude towards recording: an attitude somewhat confirmed by their third album, *Self Destruction Blues*, a collection of off-takes, singles and B-sides released late in 1982. The band persisted, however, and toured Japan early in 1983. Their fourth album, *Back To Mystery City* (with the powerful 'Malibu Beach Nightmare'), was released – again only on import – and for the first time received a lot of attention. The Rocks' gig at the Marquee in London was filmed for a video and a double live album was taped. The group set off on a "Fuck All To Do On A Saturday Night" world tour (although it proved to be a Far East jaunt again). Things were beginning to move for them, and rumours of a record deal with a major US company began to circulate.

1984 saw Hanoi Rocks' persistence paying off. CBS signed the band for a six-figure advance on a three record deal, allowing the band to shift its operations to North America. Three months were spent travelling between Toronto and New York to record the new album and Ian Hunter was brought in as lyricist for all the new material. Meanwhile their live album, *All Those Wasted Years*, together with the accompanying video, was in the shops – this time widely distributed and well received by critics and fans alike. News leaked out that the new album was to have the lyrical title of 'Silver Missiles And Nightingales', but when it appeared in July 1984 it was called *Two Steps From The Move*, a highly-polished album of uncompromising Rocks' music.

Many who have seen Hanoi Rocks live have commented that their brash and arrogant style of power rock, focused in McCoy's songs and Monroe's stage charisma, makes them the most likely successors to the Stones as the '80s progress. But the band, unrepentant hell-raisers one and all, know better. They're the new Hanoi Rocks. Accept no substitute!

Albums:

Bangkok Shocks, Saigon Shakes (1981) *Oriental Beat* (1982) *Self Destruction Blues* (1982) *Back To Mystery City* (1983) *All Those Wasted Years* (1984) *Two Steps From The Move* (1984)

Heavy Pettin

Heavy Pettin are – Steve "Hamie" Hayman (lead vocals), Gary Moat (drums), Punky Mendoza (lead guitar), Brian Waugh (bass) and Gordon Bonnar (lead guitar). They hail from Glasgow, and if you don't know them now then you soon will. That's guaranteed!

Of all the bands that have emerged in the early 80s there isn't one to have made so impressive a debut as Heavy Pettin with their *Lettin' Loose* album. Produced by Queen's Brian May (who instantly recognised the group's vast potential) it sounds like the fourth or fifth album of one of rock's biggest names, thoroughly professional, with a punch to match. Yet only three years ago Heavy Pettin were loading up their old van and travelling down into England to play a few club dates, then returning to their mums, or playing the lowlands of Scotland (not notoriously the world's Heavy Metal hunting ground). Then, in 1982, they cut a single for HM record independents, Neat.

'Roll The Dice', with its B-side 'Love Times Love' was a great success at its own level, and reached No. 5 in the UK Heavy Metal charts. More importantly, it got the attention of the media, and won the band an appearance on BBC Radio One's *Friday Rock Show* in May 1982. This exposure on Britain's largest rock radio show gave them the confidence to set up a "showcase" for the major record companies – an event where the band hires a studio for a day and then plays four or five numbers to assembled record moguls. As might have been expected, the band got several offers, and by May 1983 were in the studio with May, cutting their first album.

The speed with which things have progressed for Heavy Pettin would be surprising if not for the quality of their music. Tracks like 'Victims Of The Night' and 'Rock Me' are heavy anthems which will win them a host of fans wherever they go. In 1983 they toured Britain in style,

PHOTO SUPPLIED BY POLYDOR

supporting Ozzy Osbourne and his band. The album, released in the UK in October 1983, was out in the States in April 1984 to coincide with a tour, where Heavy Pettin were sharing a bill with Accept and Saxon. Dates with West Coast favourites Motley Crue were arranged, and a single, 'In And Out Of Love' was released in May '84 for the US market.

For Heavy Pettin it has only just begun, yet already their hard rock style with its abrasive edge has earned them the respect of fans and critics alike. Material for their second album has been written and rehearsed and the band plan to be in the studios (this time with HM expert Martin Birch) in July '84. Meanwhile they'll be recording an hour-long live video in London during the summer and preparing for an end of year tour of Japan. As I said, you may not have heard of Heavy Pettin yet. But you soon will.

Albums:
Lettin Loose (1983)

Iron Maiden

The emergence of the New Wave of British Heavy Metal occurred in the late 70s and coincided with the heyday of punk in Britain. There was nothing contradictory here, even if the hair-styles, sounds and attire of the diverging genres clashed more than a little. What punk music did was to inject a new sense of urgency and dynamics into the music, and the new heavy metal pretenders learned their lesson well. Led Zeppelin, Black Sabbath, Rainbow, Deep Purple and many other major groups who has been authentic trail-blazers were growing tired, and the upcoming generation soon incorporated the tension and life of punk into their thunderous music. Def Leppard, Saxon, Samson and Iron Maiden all broke through in the space of an eventful few months. Today, even if Def Leppard have taken a slight lead in the American market, Iron Maiden rule the roost with ferocious drive and determination.

Back in 1971, London East Ender and son of a lorry driver Steve Harris bought a Copy Fender Telecaster for forty pounds. Some years later, his thoughts turned to forming a band, and in 1975 he joined up with his friend Dave Murray, then a punk skinhead in local group Secret. Steve had failed to make his fortune in forgotten bands like Smile and Gypsy's Kiss. They recruited some other musicians who soon faded from the scene, but who had a common admiration for those pioneers of heavy metal, Deep Purple. They were soon joined by fellow East Enders Clive Burr on drums and Adrian Smith, who was playing with Urchin, on guitar. The cockney lads adopted the Iron Maiden name but failed to clinch a record deal, as their brand of music was still well out of fashion. They succeeded in scraping up enough cash to record an EP, *The Soundhouse Tapes* (named after the Soundhouse, their local pub), and pressed 5,000 copies of it on their Rock Hard label.

The now classic EP sold out in a matter of days and focussed the attention on A&R personnel on the fledgling outfit. Signed to EMI, they were soon back in the studio and given the proper means to recreate their fiery stage show. Their first album, *Iron Maiden*, was released in 1980 and the enthusiastic following their incessant gigs

had earned them flocked to the record shops and rushed the LP to number four in the British charts within weeks of its release.

The pattern was set for the years to come, with massive tours of all continents followed by dedicated time in the studio, with every album just getting bigger and bigger, both in loudness and global popularity.

Killers, recorded at London's famous Battery Studios under the supervision of ace heavy metal producer Martin Birch, a veteran of Deep Purple, Whitesnake, Rainbow and Blue Oyster Cult, managed to sell one million copies worldwide after its release in 1981. A gruelling first American tour to support the album helped it breach the American Top 60.

In 1981, following their return from the States, singer Paul Di'anno, whose new punky vocals and stable boy charm were most popular with their fans, decided to leave after a musical disagreement. Abundant rumours surrounded his departure, making newcomer Bruce Dickinson from Sheffield, who had previously fronted Samson, a controversial replacement. However, his high-pitched vocals blended in perfectly as he added new punch, and a genuine sense of harmonies thriving on emotion to the band's already lethal sound

Dickinson's first outing was again with Martin Birch at the Battery controls and the outstanding result was the *Number of the Beast* album, released in 1982, which went straight to number one in England and then spent 20 weeks in the US album charts, creeping up to number 33. The album also spawned Iron Maiden's first single hits 'Run to the Hills' (number 7) and 'Number of the Beast' (number 18), while totalling up sales of a million and a half worldwide.

Tired by the incessant touring, drummer Clive Burr then announced he was leaving the band, under the pretext of departing the music business altogether (although he re-emerged some months later in Samson). His replacement was Nicko McBrain, who had been with Trust.

The first album with the prankish and volatile McBrain was recorded in Jersey and Nassau, again with Martin Birch, as the boys in the band were now partly tax exiles, a ransom of their increasing popularity. The result was the 1982 *Piece of Mind*, another positive slice of marauding mayhem surging out of the vinyl grooves. It reached top 15 in the USA with "The Trooper" proving the hit single. Further touring naturally ensued, but Iron Maiden actually enjoy life on the road and this proves infectious for their audiences who love to share in the thrills and over-the-top extravaganzas Maiden present. The boys in Maiden actually *like* driving all day and playing every night and are not averse to 10-month, 200 show world tours embracing four continents.

Their dynamic stage show encompasses all the classic heavy metal paraphernalia: studs, leathers, tongue in cheek sexism, posing, PVC trousers so tight you can count the change in their pockets, but above all they have fun, give pleasure and make memorable records. There is always a certain scary atmosphere in their music, characterised by their mascotte Eddie, a skeletal monster who appears on all their record covers (courtesy of illustrator Derek Riggs) and makes personal appearances at crucial stages of their live show. Maiden are always on the edge but rarely go over the top. They're somewhere between high excitement and wasteful mayhem, with their trade-marked searing twin guitars and Dickinson's increasingly high-pitched vocal dramatics.

Their World Slavery tour beginning in September 1984 is another massive marathon to accompany the release of their fifth album, *Powerslave*, with a sleeve and stage production following an Egyptian theme. The mind boggles!

Albums:
Iron Maiden (1980) *Killers* (1981) *Number of the Beast* (1982) *Piece of Mind* (1983) *Powerslave* (1984)

Joan Jett

Few women have made it to the top in rock 'n' roll, let alone in the male-dominated world of heavy metal. 25 year-old Joan Jett is one, but it has been a lengthy ride full of many disappointments. There could, however, have not been any more poetic justice than the way she achieved her deserved success with a song titled 'I Love Rock 'n' Roll' – a statement of faith that has characterised Joan Jett's career.

Brought up in Baltimore, she moved to California in her mid-teens when, under the Svengali-like domination of pop legend cum entrepreneur Kim Fowley, she joined an all-girl group which he insisted on calling the Runaways. The year was 1975 and Joan – who had been a great admirer of early 70s British glitter and hard-edged rock performers like Suzi Quatro and Gary Glitter – took up her guitar playing within the group with a vengeance. The Runaways, with their carefully-manipulated jail-bait image, bridged the gap between glitter and punk.

In the Runaways, Joan played the wasted Keith Richards-role to vocalist Cherie Currie's pouting Jagger persona. Another member of the now legendary band was guitar player Lita Ford who has since emerged as a heavy metal woman of note in her own right. The group was much-maligned, but possibly ahead of its time, with the spectre of British punk and the Sex Pistols still looming over the far horizon, and their records bear witness to thin vocals and a lack of dynamics. Live, however, the Runaways were adept at setting male hearts on fire and this electric atmosphere was captured on an album recorded in Japan.

Unable to accept Fowley's machiavellian manipulations, Cherie Currie left the band (she subsequently recorded a forgettable album with her twin sister and has appeared in various B-movies), as did bass-player Jackie Fox who longed for the normal teen activities a girl her age really deserved. Joan took on the vocal mantle, but in 1979, after four albums, Fowley abandoned his creation. Lacking a record company contract and support, the Runaways parted ways. For Joan Jett, the following year proved most disheartening. She immersed herself in the murky world of Los Angeles punk with all its excesses and despair and was soon written off even by her earlier supporters. She produced an album for the Germs, after which the band's singer Darby Crash committed suicide by drug overdose. She played some sessions with former Sex Pistols Steve Jones and Paul Cook and worked on an as yet unseen rock movie, then fell ill with pneumonia and a severe heart-valve infection.

When she emerged on the scene anew, Joan had a bad reputation but, undaunted, threw herself again into recording with the assistance of manager Kenny Laguna

PHOTO: RETNA/PETER MAZEL

and writer-producer Ritchie Cordell, whom she had met whilst working on the movie. They were both veterans of the old bubblegum scene. The ensuing album *Bad Reputation*, on which Joan had enlisted her friends from the Sex Pistols and some members from Blondie, was then rejected by no less than 23 major and minor labels. Joan decided to release it independently on her own Blackhearts label. (It was eventually picked up by Boardwalk and given adequate distribution). It was a moderate success, bearing witness to Joan's spirited sense of commitment. "The album was fun for me to do. I wasn't tryin' to prove nothin'. It was a transitional album from the Runaways to a solo thing, to keep my name out there until I had a new band," says Joan.

With the assistance of Laguna, she now formed the Blackhearts with a number of obscure New York area musicians: Gary Ryan on bass, Eric Ambel (later replaced by Ricky Byrd) on guitar and Lee Crystal on drums. Following a heavy bout of touring, playing no-frills rock to growing, appreciative audiences who still remembered her

early Runaways cult-status, the band went into the studio and later emerged with the 1981 *I Love Rock 'n' Roll* album. The impact on the scene was immediate and the LP reached the Top Five while the single, in all its anthemic glory, hit the very top of the charts. Joan Jett had come back from nowhere.

The second hit from the album came with a revamped version of Tommy James' 'Crimson and Clover' which peaked at number 7, proving once and for all that Joan Jett was no one-hit wonder. A third successful hit was 'Do You Wanna Touch Me (Oh Yeah)' which reached the Top 20.

Joan Jett's insistence on rock 'n' roll's integrity was finally paying off and even her first album rebounded into the charts on the strength of her singles successes. Her voice was by now deeper than the little girl tones of the Runaways' days and her black leather-clad stage presence and bad girl wearing tons of eye liner image caught the public's imagination. A gruelling programme of world-wide touring helped her spread her hard rock gospel and gritty videos, directed by David Mallett, have now made her a household name in rock circles.

Following the death of owner Neil Bogart, Boardwalk folded and the release of her next album, simply called *Album* was delayed while she and her management netogiated a new deal with MCA. Her videos are now staple diet on MTV but Joan has lost none of her toughness and street credibility. Her story has been called a Cinderella one by many journalists, but Joan Jett is unique and continues a career that has never been influenced by style or passing fashions. The girl has guts.

Albums:
Bad Reputation (1980) *I Love Rock 'n' Roll* (1981) *Album* (1983)

Journey

For a band who were once termed faceless (alongside REO Speedwagon, Foreigner, Rush and Styx) in a now notorious article in *Rolling Stone*, Journey can not only laugh all the way to the bank but also ripost with a roll call of musicians whose individual talents almost map the history of modern rock in America.

Their manager, a portly guy by the name of Walter 'Herbie' Herbert, is very much the sixth member of the group and explains their successful philosophy: "I didn't want to work with anybody who didn't have the common goal that we could all share, and our common denominator was this – we wanted to make a contribution to the state of the art on every level. We wanted to be the best songwriters, best players, best singers, best entertainers . . . We wanted to have the best personnel, best staging, we wanted to have the best sounding records and the best packaged records. We wanted to do everything right! And not miss a trick. And that's what we applied ourselves to from the first day." A policy which has taken Journey from modest beginnings to the very top, as arch-heroes of the Stadium rock genre.

Back in 1973, Herbert envisioned an all-star San Francisco band, not unlike the acclaimed Muscle Shoals studio aces. He had managed a band called Frumious Bandersnatch in the 60s which included Ross Valory on bass and George Tickner on guitar. After the band's demise, Valory worked with Steve Miller and Herbert began an association with the Santana management. This is where he first came across teenage guitar genius Neil Schon and keyboards player and singer Gregg Rolie. When Santana went through one of its periodic reshuffles, it was Herbert who suggested that Schon and Rolie should join up with Valory and Tickner to form a new band. Prairie Prince, then with the Tubes, momentarily joined on drums but soon found himself unable to commit himself full-time to Journey.

After trying out over 30 unsuitable drummers, the band persuaded legendary British session man Aynsley Dunbar, then living on the US West Coast, to join them and they signed up with Columbia Records in November 1974. Their first album, *Journey* appeared in April 1975. Shortly after, George Tickner left the group, unable to cope with

the touring. Two further albums, *Look Into The Future* (January 1976) and *Next* (January 1977) followed and enjoyed mild chart success, the last one inching its way up to number 77 in the US album charts. The steady touring saw Journey gain many fans with their grandiose and loud art rock techno-flash, but something was still missing.

It was producer Roy Thomas Baker, who had turned the band down several times, who convinced them to look for a first-class vocalist (Rolie had until then taken vocal duties from behind his keyboards). Robert Fleischman briefly assumed frontman role in 1977 but didn't last. Finally, Steve Perry from Hanford, California, previously with the Alien Project, moved in and Baker accepted handling Journey in the studio for what was to be their breakthrough album, *Infinity*.

Released in February 1978, the album was an instant hit and reached number 21 in the charts. Despite this welcome success, Aynsley Dunbar became dissatisfied with the band's musical evolution and left, to be replaced by Steve Smith who had previously worked with Ronnie Montrose. The new line-up was to remain together for a further two years during which Journey attained platinum status with *Evolution* and *Departure*. They also enjoyed their first singles hits during this period: 'Lovin', Touchin', Squeezin'' and 'Any Way You Want It'. All the hard work and planning by Herbert were at last bearing fruit.

Following the consolidation of a compilation collection, *In The Beginning* and double live set *Captured* which reached the number nine spot (only one rung lower than the studio-bound *Departure*), Gregg Rolie departed, tired of the constant touring. He was replaced by Jonathan Cain, previously with the Babys. This was the final ingredient in Journey's unceasing voyage to the top and the first album recorded with this final line-up spawned the mega-platinum, chart-topping album *Escape* and single 'Who's Cryin' Now' (number four), itself soon bettered by the number three position of 'Open Arms'.

Jonathan Cain's pop sensibility, allied with the drive of Perry and Schon's quicksilver guitar runs made Journey the darlings of the American radio airwaves and their wide popularity was maximised through a highly professional policy of touring on a large scale. A 72-date tour in late 1981 and another in 1982 reached an estimated two and a half million people.

This huge success continued unabated in 1983 with *Frontiers*, 'Separate Ways' and 'Faithfully' notching up top 20 status with ease. On a separate front, the clever merchandising of the band scored another innovative first with a video game based on the *Escape* album! But the scale of Journey's success, though unequalled by most other American hard rock bands, has not deflected its musicians from their quest for perfection and to avoid falling into a familiar, if commercial rut, many of the band's members have also been active with individual projects. Schon has made two jazz-oriented albums with keyboard virtuoso Jan Hammer, Steve Perry has done a solo album and Jonathan Cain has written most of the songs and produced an album for his wife, Tané Cain.

The band has now been going for over ten years but the future holds no fear for Journey. Jonathan Cain says: "I'm really confident that we're going to come up with some extraordinary music. We're going to become innovators. I hope our music becomes cinematic, like a new soundtrack. We're more than a rock 'n' roll band."

Albums

Journey (1975) *Look Into The Future* (1976) *Next* (1977) *Infinity* (1978) *Evolution* (1979) *Departure* (1980) *In The Beginning* (1980)* *Captured* (1981) *Escape* (1981) *Frontiers* (1983)

*Compilation album.

Judas Priest

They come from Birmingham in the industrial kernel of Britain, a thriving scene that has also spawned major names like Black Sabbath, Led Zeppelin, ELO and many others. They've come a long way since then and are now poised for total metal domination defenders of the metal faith and craftsmen of mayhem. But they still remember the early days when they built up their muscles by hauling all their equipment from gig to gig.

The origins of the band go back a long way and, sadly, no one has survived from the original line-up, when Judas Priest flirted dangerously with pop. In 1973, singer Rob Halford and bass player Ian Hill joined the group and imitated the aggressive metal stance that was soon to become so characteristic. In 1974, the band signed its first recording contract and guitarists K. K. Downing and

Glenn Tipton and drummer John Hinch joined. This initial line-up recorded a debut album, *Rocka Rolla*, with producer Rodger Bain, released in 1974 to few waves of instant recognition.

Hinch left the band shortly before they signed to Columbia/CBS, a major label, and was replaced by Alan Moore for the recording of Judas Priest's second album, *Sad Wings of Destiny*, which appeared in 1976. But the drum position remained unsatisfactory and Moore left soon afterwards. Simon Phillips, an experienced session drummer was recruited for the recording of *Sin After Sin*, under the production guidance of Roger Glover of Rainbow. The album confirmed the band's gradual progress and steady touring in England and Europe followed, honing the group's dynamic stage presence.

PHOTO: C.B.S./PAUL COX

Les Binks, a drummer who had previously played with Eric Burdon, was taken aboard and played on the 1978 album *Stained Class*. This attempt saw Judas Priest breaking into the US charts for the first time. The next album, *Killing Machine* (titled *Hell Bent For Leather* in the US), confirmed Judas Priest's rising stature in America with the success of 'Take On The World'. The raw edge and aggressiveness of the band that made their live show so increasingly popular was captured on a live set, *Unleashed in the East*, recorded in Japan, which broke through into the American Top One Hundred. But the constant touring was too much for Les Binks, who left the band, physically and mentally exhausted by the unending rigors of the road. Once again, Judas Priest were drummerless; it was becoming too much of a habit!

Enter Dave Holland. The energetic drummer acted as a catalyst and the first album he appeared on, *British Steel* reached the Top 40 and spawned hit singles with 'Living After Midnight' and 'Breaking the Law'.

Priest had finally made it after solid years of hard graft and the following albums just kept on ascending the charts and gaining the band new fans: *Point Of Entry* was the 1981 offering, and *Screaming For Vengeance* in 1982 (produced by Tom Allom) unleashed the expected superstardom as it went platinum with a vengeance, selling over two million copies. The 1984 *Defenders of the Faith*, recorded in Ibiza and mixed in Maimi, again by Allom, confirmed the mega-status of the band, a prominent position they are likely to retain for much time to come.

Judas Priest and blond leather-clad singer Rob Halford give the fans what they want and more. A rampaging quintet of metal marauders, they offer music and fun in a big way. This is heavy metal by the book, full of originality, fluency of dynamics and consistent delivery. The Priest stage show is one of the most flashy, trashy and over the top extravaganzas that fans can witness – almost the HM equivalent of the Royal Wedding. Almost every visual cliché imaginable is used: sky-high drum-riser, hydraulic platforms Strobe lights, flashbombs, smoke and dry ice billowing from floor and ceiling, major futuristic centre-pieces and, of course, the inevitable motorbike . . . An unforgettable metal kaleidoscope.

"The thing about Judas Priest," says K.K., "is that it's pure energy as a unit, as a force and, although we do take it seriously, it's something to be enjoyed in a light-hearted way rather than a serious way." Nevertheless, the band have a strong commitment to their music.

As Halford puts it: "Our faith is heavy metal music. And we're defending it against every aspect: from the people that knock it, and from ever going out of style and fashion, which we never think will happen anyway . . . It's such a gutsy, raw musical expression that it reaches everybody. I'd personally like to take heavy metal to every country in the world, although that might not be possible. It's such a great attraction to people, and let's hope governments allow it . . . It's a limitless form of music and it's going to be around for so many years. It's going to be around at least until I drop dead – it's got a hell of a long time to go.'"

With a credo like that, heavy metal is in good hands.

Albums:

Rocka Rolla (1974) *Sad Wings of Destiny* (1976) *Sin After Sin* (1977) *Stained Class* (1978) *The Best of Judas Priest* (1978) *Killing Machine* (*Hell Bent for Leather*, in the US) (1979) *Unleashed in the East* (1979) *British Steel* (1980) *Point of Entry* (1981) *Screaming For Vengeance* (1982) *Defenders of the Faith* (1984)

PHOTO: L.F.I./SIMON FOWLER

Kiss

Kiss were formed in New York in 1972 when bassist Gene Simmons and guitarist Paul Stanley formed a trio with drummer Peter Criss. They soon discovered they were lacking vocal punch and advertised in The Village Voice for a vocalist/guitarist. Ace Frehley answered, joined the band, and . . .

Well, nothing might have happened. Sharing a drafty 23rd Street (Manhattan) loft, the band rehearsed and rehearsed, and, for a meagre return, worked the New York clubs circuit. And so it might have stayed, with Kiss no more famous than Rainbow or Wicked Lester, the bands Simmons and Stanley had played in previously, but with Ace's arrival something crystallized and the band began to experiment with make-up and characters and, in June 1973, went into the studios to cut a demo tape of five rock numbers; five tracks which ultimately appeared on their first album. Even so, they might have remained a fairly obscure hard rock act had not entrepreneur Bill Aucoin (producer of the TV rock show *Flipside*) seen the band, liked what he saw, and offered them a lucrative deal as their manager. Within months they had a recording contract and, under Aucoin's wing, the band developed their visual image and took the show on the road.

With their individualised grease-paint masks (Simmons as "Demon", Stanley as "Lover") they became comic-book heroes and villains, garishly dressed and instantly recognisable. Their visual impact was further enhanced by a stage show which had exploding balls of fire, rocket-firing guitars, revolving lights and police sirens and a fully-mobile special effects stage. It was something entirely different, rock 'n' roll theatre writ large, and when bassist Simon spat blood or swallowed great gobbets of flame the ever-growing audiences would go berserk.

Aucoin took Kiss from the total obscurity of being part-time musicians holding down dead-end jobs to platinum-earning megastars – and all in the space of three years. Which is not to say that it was all hype, for the band's potential was there all the time. There was no real secret to their success; it was hard work all the way. They toured America solidly throughout the rest of 1973 and the whole of 1974, playing practically every night. And while the critics saw only the face-paint and the over-the-top theatrics, generally loathing Kiss, the fans lapped up the hard rock music and the larger-than-life fantasy of their stage act. Kiss' first album, on the new Casablanca label, was called simply *Kiss* and was a quality hard rock outing, providing many of the favourites of a decade later. Its immediate sales impact in February 1974 was small by comparison to what was to happen later, but it sold sufficiently well to allow the band to release (after a further eight months gruelling touring) a second album, *Hotter*

Than Hell, just as heavy as their debut but perhaps a bit stronger in the melody department. Album No. 3 was *Dressed To Kill,* released in March 1975, perhaps the best Kiss album of those early years, with the hard rocking 'Rock And Roll All Nite' as its most memorable cut.

Image apart, though, Kiss were just another eccentric heavy band back in the summer of 1975. They were already developing their cult fan club, the Kiss Army, as it came to be known, but outside of those few hundred thousand fanatics Kiss were seen as shallow poseurs. All of that changed with the release of their first live album in September 1975. *Kiss Alive* is a double set which, for Casablanca Records, was a make-or-break venture. They made it, and in some style! It went gold, and from it Kiss had their first hit single, a live version of 'Rock And Roll All Nite' which went to No. 12 in the US singles chart in November that year. It was the first of eight top forty singles Kiss were to have during the seventies. From there on there was no looking back. Every album went instant gold, the majority going on to earn platinum discs (15 gold, 11 platinum was their US tally at the end of 1983, with in excess of 50 million albums sold worldwide, more than any other group during the seventies!).

The music was hard and heavy, the lyrics often crude but never less than effective in conveying the band's blatant sexuality. There was a slight softening of their sound after *Alive,* with orchestras and choirs on *Destroyer,* but with *Rock And Roll Over,* released in November 1976, they were back to raw rock with few frills. The trend of *Destroyer* (towards sophistication of production and a greater commercial feel) was dominant in the next album, *Love Gun,* which went platinum on its release in June 1977, but Kiss were still the definitive Heavy Metal heroes of the USA. 'Beth', their 1976 single, was their first Top Ten hit, reaching No. 7 in September and staying in the top forty for 13 weeks. By this time Kiss were so big in the States that Marvel issued a Kiss comic, which sold in excess of 400,000 copies (some estimates say 700,000!). The band became the heroes of a far wider (and far younger) audience, and the Kiss Army swelled its ranks in excess of 100,000. A second live album, *Alive II* appeared in October 1977 and proved even more successful than the first. Then, in the latter half of 1978, the band engaged in a number of projects; a feature-length cartoon film called *Kiss Meets The Phantom Of The Park,* a second Marvel Kiss comic and four solo albums, released simultaneously on September 18th 1978.

The decline of Kiss in the late '70s may well date from the release of the solo albums. None of them sold as well as expected, and whilst Paul Stanley's was perhaps the most interesting, it was Ace Frehley's album which eventually

did best in terms of sales.

In May 1979, *Dynasty* (Die – Nasty!) appeared, from which came another hit single, 'I Was Made For Lovin' You', which got to No. 11 in June that year. But then, following the release of *Unmasked* (perhaps the weakest of all Kiss' group albums) in May 1980, Peter Criss left the band to pursue a solo career. Kiss decided to re-assess their image, moving away from their glam image towards something softer and more 'New Romantic' – a move which coincided with their poppier music. The session drummer on *Unmasked*, Anton Fig, was not retained by the group, however, and Kiss brought in Eric Carr. Their first project with Carr was *The Elder*, a concept album, featuring some songs by Lou Reed. When it appeared in November 1981, however, it proved the poorest selling Kiss album since the early days, and the film it was written for never materialized. Realizing their mistake, perhaps (as Kiss Army fans deserted by the platoon), the group reverted to its more familiar aspect – face-masks and heavy metal music, and did far better with *Killers* in 1982 (a mixture of old songs re-worked and some new material). But it was not until the release of *Creatures Of The Night* in late 1982 that Kiss re-affirmed their position as one of the leading American HM bands.

Creatures Of The Night was harder and heavier and more intense than anything Kiss had ever done before, and it won back hosts of the HM fans they'd lost whilst wooing the teenybopper hordes. It was also the last album to feature Ace Frehley, who eventually went on to form his own band, Frehley's Comet, in May 1984. After audition-ing numerous musicians, Kiss settled on guitarist Vinnie Vincent, who played on much of the *Creatures* material and toured with the band in early 1983 to promote the album – a tour which culminated in a huge concert in Brazil in front of 300,000 South American Kiss fans. This new line-up returned to the States to record *Lick It Up*, released in late 1983.

In January 1984 guitarist Vincent was fired and then rehired, but by May he was out for good and Mark Norton was in. Face paint was also out. *Lick It Up* had finally unmasked the group after a decade behind face paint, and the "Lick It Up" tour (featuring their stage 'tank') was a slightly different, but by no means less exciting Kiss. The Norton/Carr/Stanley/Simmons Kiss have now completed their new album, *Animalize,* and, more than ten years on from their debut, they seem as enthusiastic, heavy and outrageous as ever. Love It Loud? They sure do!

Albums

Kiss (1974) *Hotter Than Hell* (1974) *Dressed To Kill* (1975) *Alive* (1975) *Destroyer* (1976) *Rock And Roll Over* (1976) *Love Gun* (1977) *Alive II* (1977) *Double Platinum* (1978)* *Gene Simmons* (1978) *Paul Stanley* (1978) *Ace Frehley* (1978) *Peter Criss* (1978) *Best Of Solo Albums* (1978)* *Dynasty* (1979) *Unmasked* (1980) *Music From 'The Elder'* (1981) *Killers* (1982)* *Creatures Of The Night* (1982) *Lick It Up* (1983) *Animalize* (1984)

*Compilation albums.

Krokus

Formed in 1974 by bassist Chris Von Rohr, Krokus are one of the more unlikely bands on the heavy metal circuit, hailing from Switzerland, more famed for yodelling than heavy rock assault. But with six albums released and a seventh in the can, Krokus are set to break through into the big time in the States; their last album, *Head Hunter*, sold close on half a million copies there.

It seems a long way from the time when the band (ignored in Britain and the States), toured Europe laying down a grass-roots following, particularly in Spain. Two albums originated from this period, *Pay It In Metal* and *Painkillers*, but it was only with their third album, *Metal Rendezvous*, released in 1980, that Krokus found a wider, non-European audience for their crisp, hard-edged sound

with its melodic lines. At this time the band consisted of Von Rohr, Fernando Von Arb on lead guitar and vocals, Tommy Keiffer on rhythm guitar and vocals, Juerg Naegeli on keyboards and Freddy Steady on drums. Von Rohr decided to shed Naegeli's keyboard sound and brought in Maltese-born Marc Storace on lead vocals. It was Storace's presence that focused the music and attracted new attention to the band. *Metal Rendezvous* sold 100,000 copies in the States, charted in the UK and encouraged Krokus to take their exciting live act on tour in both countries.

After recording a new album, *Hardware*, Keiffer left the band and was replaced by Armand (Mandy) Meier. The new album did even better than the last and Krokus launched a 20-date US tour early in 1982 to promote the album. By the end of the year, US and European tours completed, a new album, *One Vice At A Time* recorded, Krokus were in the top league of Heavy Metal acts. Mark Kohler joined them on rhythm guitar for the new album, replacing Meier.

1982 saw Krokus heading out on a World tour, recording a new album, *Head Hunter*, changing drummers (Steve Pace in, Freddy Steady out) and generally building on their by now considerable reputation as a powerful, high-energy rock band. Nonetheless, the success of *Head Hunter*, released in 1983, was phenomenal considering the initial response of the States to Krokus. The band was chosen to support Def Leppard on their Stateside tour and, despite severe disagreements between the two bands (and fisticuffs between their two managers!), Krokus were at last playing to 20,000 audiences and getting the attention their music deserved.

Back from the States, Krokus made several changes in their line-up. Out were Steve Pace, founder Chris Von Rohr and Mark Kohler. In were Jeff Klayven on drums, Patrick Mason on rhythm guitar and – Mark Kohler again, but this time on bass! Mason stayed only a few months before the band were down to a four-piece again when, in the Spring of 1984 they went into the studio to cut a new album, tentatively called *Midnight Maniac*.

At the time of writing Krokus are leading a European Heavy Metal movement (that includes bands like Vandenberg and Hanoi Rocks) which is beginning to influence and change the traditional USA–UK dominance of the form. They can only get bigger!

Albums:
Pay It In Metal (1977) *Painkillers* (1978) *Metal Rendezvous* (1980) *Hardware* (1981) *One Vice At A Time* (1982) *Head Hunter* (1983)

PHOTO: L.F.I./MICHAEL PUTLAND

Led Zeppelin

When, in July 1968, Keith Relf and Jim McCarty quit the highly successful British group the Yardbirds, they left their guitarist, Jimmy Page, with the problem of forming a group to fulfil their commitment to tour Scandinavia. Page's first choices for the New Yardbirds were singer Terry Reid, drummer B. J. Wilson and pianist Nicky Hopkins, but none of them were interested. Reid suggested a 20-year old singer, Robert Plant, who was in a Midlands-based semi-pro band, Band Of Joy. Plant in turn recommended fellow B.O.J. drummer John Bonham, who was also recruited. The fourth member was found in session musician John Paul Jones, who had worked with Page on Donovan's 'Hurdy Gurdy Man' single. The four musicians clicked immediately and on completing their Scandinavian tour went straight into the studios to cut their first album. It took them 15 hours and a maximum of two takes per track, the intention being to get "as near a live sound as possible". Who drummer Keith Moon suggested that they re-name the group "lead balloon", because that's how they'd go down in Britain at that time. The band changed that slightly, re-named themselves Led Zeppelin and looked towards the States.

Led Zeppelin, released in February 1969, was and is an astonishing album. From the opening of 'Good Times Bad Times' through to the final bars of 'How Many More Times', it was a classic. The group had taken blues influences and re-shaped them, creating a form of hard rock which, in its dynamics, was different from any that preceded it. The conception is Jimmy Page's, but the group playing is pure Zeppelin, right from the start. The tour of the States which promoted the album was a huge success and the album went gold very quickly. Advance orders for the second album were equally astonishing – 400,000! – and when it came out later that year, it proved even better than the first. Within two months it hit the No. 1 spot in the US charts and stayed in the top five for the next five months.

Against the band's wishes the opening track on *Led Zeppelin II*, 'Whole Lotta Love' (perhaps the best known heavy riff ever) was released as a single and reached No. 4 in the US singles charts in December 1969. Four big tours of the States during 1969 had made the band one of the biggest attractions in rock music. Within a year Zeppelin had conquered the most lucrative market in the world, created two of rock music's seminal albums, and won platinum discs for everything they'd released. Statistically it was impressive, though not half as impressive as the music on *Zeppelin II*, which showed the band moving away from its blues roots and beginning to diversify, Robert Plant having a hand in all the compositions (he wrote nothing on the debut album) and giving the band its

distinctive lyrical sound. Zeppelin's immaculate, instinctive sense of timing – their ability to switch from acoustic simplicity to heavy riffing in the space of a bar – was unique in rock music and influenced numerous bands over the next decade (Rush in particular). Tracks like 'Thank You' and 'Ramble On' demonstrated a romantic side to Zeppelin which was to blossom on *Led Zeppelin III*, released in late 1970.

Zeppelin's fifth tour of the States in March/April 1970 grossed over a million dollars, and their headlining appearance at the Bath Festival in England saw then play in front of a 150,000 crowd. 'Immigrant Song' from *III* was released as a single in the States and climbed to No. 16. The new album was markedly less heavy than its predecessors, but no less popular for that.

Folk influences had shaped *Led Zeppelin III*, and were to have their impact on two tracks from the fourth album, the untitled "Runes" album, which appeared late in 1971. 'The Battle Of Evermore' had Plant duetting with folk-singer Sandy Denny, while 'Stairway To Heaven' (which was to become the band's anthem) mixed folk and heavy influences to create one of rock music's few genuinely brilliant songs; a song which seems to embrace all that was best in Zeppelin.

After the hectic touring of '69 and '70, the band had slowed down and when they toured the States in 1972 (playing an incredible four-hour set), followed by Europe and Britain, they broke attendance records wherever they went. But perhaps the most impressive concert was in Tampa, Florida on May 5th, 1973, when they played to 56,800 people, the largest audience for a single artist performance in history. In live performance terms they were bigger than the Beatles.

March 1973 also saw the release of their fifth album, *Houses Of The Holy*, containing 'D'yer Maker' (Jamaica), a reggae track, which, as a single, reached No. 20 in the US charts. But Zeppelin weren't losing their direction, as tracks like 'No Quarter' and 'The Rain Song' proved. Like all their albums it went platinum in weeks (in Germany it won a pre-release gold record), but the music press, for so long on Zeppelin's side, carped at the new album. The band's response was simple; they ignored the media and went to the fans. Over a million people saw their 34-date American tour, paying over 3 million dollars. But in 1974 the band kept a low-profile, working on their film (*The Song Remains The Same*, which finally appeared in 1976) and on their sixth album. At the same time they left Atlantic and formed their own record company, Swan Song.

Physical Graffiti, released in January 1975, was platinum before its release and went to No. 1 on both sides of the Atlantic immediately. In fact, so popular were Zeppelin that all six Zeppelin albums could be found in the Billboard charts (a first for any artist) on March 25th, 1975. The double album contained some material left over from previous albums (i.e. 'The Rover', recorded for the fourth album); it was an eye-opener to some, a disappointment to others. There was nothing comparable to 'Stairway To Heaven' or 'Whole Lotta Love', but there was the epic 'Kashmir' and the plaintive 'Ten Years Gone' to satisfy Zeppelin fans.

Presence was the next Zeppelin album, released early in 1976, and contained a new classic, 'Achilles' Last Stand', a heavy rocker in the old mould. But the album had been recorded in the face of Robert Plant's recovery from a car crash in the summer of 1975, and the old Zeppelin zest seems missing from the album.

In October 1976 Zeppelin at long last premiered their film, *The Song Remains The Same*, releasing a live double album at the same time. Again (as for *Presence*) the album went to No. 1 both sides of the Atlantic and earned further platinum discs worldwide, this time deservedly, for the album is a showcase of the band's live act. 'Stairway To Heaven', 'No Quarter' and the 27-minute version of 'Dazed And Confused' are the album's highlights, giving a glimpse of Zeppelin circa 1973. 1977 saw the band touring the States again, but the sudden death of Plant's son ended the tour abruptly. Rumours of a split began to circulate.

After a long break the band returned in August 1979, with a new album. *In Through The Out Door*, and their first concert in the UK since 1975. It was August 4th, and 270,000 people made the trip to Knebworth to see the band, whose set took in twenty three songs from all eight albums. It was the last time they were to be seen in the UK, for in the midst of planning an American tour, in September 1980 John Bonham died from inhaling his own vomit after a heavy drinking session. The announcement of the group's demise which followed in December ended the career of the most successful group since the Beatles.

Coda, released in January 1983, was a collection of eight previously unreleased tracks, including a delightful version of 'I Can't Quit You Baby', recorded at a sound rehearsal in January 1970. It reached No. 6 in the US album charts, marking the end of an era. Robert Plant has gone on to a successful solo career, and there were rumours of Page and Plant linking with Alan White and Chris Squire of Yes to form XYZ, but nothing came of it. Meanwhile the albums remain, perhaps some of the most influential albums in rock's history. For which, in Robert Plant's memorable stage-phrase, Eye Thank Yew.

Albums:

Led Zeppelin (1969) *Led Zeppelin II* (1969) *Led Zeppelin III* (1970) *Led Zeppelin IV* (1971) *Houses Of The Holy* (1973) *Physical Graffiti* (1975) *Presence* (1976) *The Song Remains The Same* (1976) *In Through The Out Door* (1979) *Coda* (1982)

Mama's Boys

Ireland doesn't produce that much rock music for the international marketplace, but what it does allow out beyond its shores is usually of the very highest quality – U2, Gary Moore, Thin Lizzy, Horslips. And now there's Mama's Boys, worthy successors to the heavier of those names, a band who, curiously enough, began as a traditional folk outfit. In fact, until late in the '70s Mama's Boys hadn't even heard of heavy rock music. That was, until the day they found themselves on the same festival bill as Southern Ireland's rock heroes, Horslips.

You'll be forgiven if you've not read of Horslips in the annals of Heavy Metal, but for a moment just imagine the impact on the three-brother folk group, Mama's Boys. Here, in Horslips, was a group steeped in traditional Irish folk tunes, yet who played electric instruments and could rock like Thin Lizzy on a hot night. The youngsters had never dreamed such a sound was possible. In no time at all they were playing Horslips covers in their act, catching up

with the heavy rock scene (and AC/DC seem to have made a special impact on them), and beginning to formulate their own brand of heavy metal.

Mama's Boys, the McManus brothers, are Pat, 24 (guitar and fiddle), John, 22 (bass and vocals), and Tommy, 17 (drums); being brothers, their playing has an instinctive tightness that so few bands ever acquire (ZZ Top are an obvious comparison here) and a heaviness that belies their folk origins. They are also workaholics and have managed to fit in a staggering 300-gigs-a-year schedule in their first few years, at first in Ireland, then, in 1981, following the release of their first, self-financed album, *Official Bootleg*, in England, supporting Hawkwind.

From the start the rock critics gave rave reviews, especially for their high energy, rivetting live performances. Pat's guitar and violin playing (he owes his nickname, 'The Professor' to his rapid and intelligent technique) drew especial attention, though it was as a unit, as

PHOTO SUPPLIED BY JIVE

Mama's Boys, that they really shone – as a six-armed rocker named McManus! Two more albums emerged, *Plug It In* and *Turn It Up,* each revealing the band's fast development into one of the most powerful and interesting HM bands about – a subtle band with the occasional bluesy touch and a kick like a steel donkey. They toured with Wishbone Ash, then, early in 1983, with veteran Irish rockers Thin Lizzy, winning fans wherever they went.

1984 began well for Mama's Boys. Their European tour, supporting Germany's all-conquering Scorpions, was an unqualified success, whilst their latest album, *Mama's Boys,* is their most accomplished and entertaining yet, providing a hit single, 'Mama We're All Crazy Now' (a cover of Slade's hit), as well as new Mama's Boys classics like 'Crazy Daisy's House of Dreams' (so melodic *and* so heavy!) and the delightful slow blues, 'Lonely Soul'. It's a performance that's certain to win them a whole host of new fans.

Albums:

Official Bootleg (1982) *Plug It In* (1982) *Turn It Up* (1983) *Mama's Boys* (1984)

Metal America

Whatever happened to Randy Holden? I ask myself that question whenever I ponder the beginnings of Heavy Metal in the States, because it seems to sum up something about the vastness of the music scene in the USA. That such an excellent heavy musician can appear, produce such superb heavy music (Side Two of Blue Cheer's 1969 outing, *New Improved!*, to be precise) and then disappear again indicates just how large the field is – and how small the individual musician. It also reminds me that so much American hard rock – some of it of excellent quality – never even leaves the State, let alone gets abroad, and that's a great shame. Blue Cheer, of course, did make it abroad in the late sixties, along with Grand Funk, the Amboy Dukes (Ted Nugent's Amboy Dukes, to be specific!), the MC5, the Doors (don't forget who wrote 'Roadhouse Blues'!), early Jefferson Airplane (just listen to their live stuff) and many more. A wide variety of heavy music appeared in the States in the late sixties and early seventies – sounds which shaped American metal in a specific way, making it more melodic, more hook-orientated and less riff-based than its British counterpart. Then, in the early and mid seventies came Alice Cooper, the New York Dolls, Kiss – the whole Glam-rock trip. Heavy *and* outrageous. Theatrical. Abusive and highly offensive to the moral majority. And again these were influences which, ten years on, have made their indelible mark on American heavy metal – specifically on the LA scene. Which is not, of course, to forget Canada and the HM scene which developed (as it seemed) out of Rush's one-band-crusade to put Canada on the Heavy Metal map . . .

Here, then, is a guide to some of those bands who soaked up the influences, refurbished them and, in the late seventies and early eighties, formed a new generation of Heavy Metal/Hard Rock. And if it seems at times that they all come from either LA or Toronto . . . well, that's the way it is at present. Those two centres are currently vying with England's industrial Midlands for the title of **THE** Heavy Metal centre of the world (is it something in the water?).

First on the alphabetical list of second leaguers is **LEE AARON**, a 22-year old Canadian female vocalist whose 1982 debut album, *Lee Aaron* was produced by (and features) Triumph's Rik Emmett. She's a powerful, raunchy singer with a strong HM backing band. In Canada she had a 60-minute TV special devoted to her music.

ALDO NOVA is both vocalist and leader of the band named after him, a charismatic singer whose second album, *Subject* (1983) went gold in the States. Touring with a 5-man back-up, he's far heavier live than on record.

ANGEL are a late seventies band who had six albums out between 1975 and 1980, folded, and then reformed very recently to pick up where they'd left off. A five-man group dominated by keyboards and vocals, they were on Casablanca, Kiss's label, before they split in 1980. What they play is essentially metal-pop, but it can be *White Hot*, like their 1977 album.

ANTHRAX sound more like a British band than most US groups, playing a speedy high-energy metal that's somewhat similar to Metallica. They're a five-man band from New York, fronted by vocalist Neil Turbin. Their debut album, *Fistful Of Metal* (1984) shows them to be a most promising prospect.

ANVIL are perhaps the best known of the new Canadian acts and, as their *Forged In Fire* album proves, they're specialists at a kind of musical lobotomy. This is one band that can claim to be free of Rush's influence, anyway!

BLACK'N'BLUE may be part of the LA scene, but they come from Portland, Oregon (so, strictly speaking, they're still a West Coast band). They're a five-piece who started up in 1982 and have a slight pop orientation. Their debut album, *Black'n'Blue* appeared in 1984.

BON JOVI may well (along with Aldo Nova) be the first of these 'also-mentioned' acts to graduate to the big time. He's a 22-year old singer/songwriter from New Jersey who was opening for ZZ Top at Madison Square Gardens as a 19-year old, long before he got a record contract. *Bon Jovi*, his 1984 release, made the US top 100, its melodic but powerful, hard-edged Heavy Metal style (with good harmonies and excellent guitar work) proves that he's chosen his backing band well.

CONEY HATCH are another Canadian band who have recently graduated from the club circuit. They're a four-man team with two guitars and *Outta Hand* (1983), their second album, is a first-rate PURE Heavy Metal.

THE ERIC MARTIN BAND comes from San Fransisco, although Eric Martin himself is a native of Sacramento. The band was originally called 415 and had a very sub-Journeyesque sound. They're still a harmony group with soul influences, but their new sound is much harder and sharper. Their debut album was *Sucker For A Pretty Face* (1983).

THE GODZ are a semi-legendary four-piece who were formed in 1975, made two albums and then split up, reforming again in 1981. Despite a three year break they have made a strong come back and are still one of the most exciting live bands to be seen. Their second album, *Nothing Is Sacred,* is a good introduction to their hard sound.

GREAT WHITE are another band from Los Angeles, a four-piece fronted by vocalist Jack Russell. They released a mini-LP in 1983, followed up by *Great White* in 1984.

HELIX are a Saxon-style HM band from Canada – a

PHOTO: FRASER GRAY

five-man outfit with dual guitars. Their album *No Rest For The Wicked* (1983) is standard-but-good metal fare.

HELLION are an LA band who are winning a growing underground following. They finance all their own projects, including their debut album, *Hellion* (1984). Fronted by attractive vocalist Anne Boleyn, Hellion provide true Heavy Metal (non-Glam!) with style. And Boleyn can scream to make Gillan envious!

Arizona seems an unlikely enough place for an Americanized version of Judas Priest to spring from, but 5-piece Motley Crue-look-alikes **ICON** hail from that deserted State.

KILLER DWARFS deserve mention if only to state that Bryce, Darrell, Russell and Angelo all sport the surname Dwarf. They're strong Canadian rockers – a dirty guitar-dominated group.

LEGS DIAMOND are another of those bands who have been encouraged to re-form after the recent upsurge in Metal interest in the States. Their debut album, *Legs Diamond*, appeared in 1977, and three members of the five-piece that folded in 1979 are in the new group, whose excellent mini-LP, *Out On Bail* came out in 1984. Unsurprisingly, they come from LA, but their music isn't in the fashionable glam-Metal vein, but is enjoyable, gutsy, high-energy riff-laden hard rock. Good stuff!

The interest in Sword-and-Sorcery gimmickry has flourished mainly amongst the British HM bands, but **MANOWAR**, a four-piece from New York have gained a reputation for doom-laden imagery in their music and stage act. They're a loud volume thrash band, definitely non-Glam, and are seen by most US fans (mistakenly, of

course) as an English band. They're also one of the loudest bands in the world, touching 160 decibels regularly (that's louder than Concorde landing!). *Sign Of The Hammer* was their 1984 album.

Another fast-speed non-glam thrash band is **METALLICA** who have moved up to San Fransisco from LA. They supported Krokus when they toured the States in 1982 and produced their debut album, *Kill 'Em All*. in 1983. They're definitely European-influenced and cite Motorhead as their heroes.

NIGHT RANGER are a loud, melodic heavy rock band from San Fransisco who can boast one of the finest guitarists in the States. Brad Gillis (his guitar-partner in Night Ranger is the talented Jeff Watson) was Ozzy Osbourne's guitarist on *Talk Of The Devil*. They've been going since 1980, but Gillis joined in late '82. *Dawn Patrol* was their magnificent debut in 1982, followed by *Midnight Madness* in 1983. This five-piece can't possibly stay small for long.

QUEENSRYCHE are from Seattle and are a 6-man heavy thrash band. They're currently recording their debut album, but will be seen in the UK when they support Dio on their tour in September/October 1984.

The LA Glam-rock scene is presently *very* fashionable. It's the thing, and **RATT**, muscular and macho poseurs that they are, are a hot, upcoming act with a huge following in LA. This five-piece band produced their first full album, *Out Of The Cellar* in 1984.

THE RODS are famous for their extra-curricular activities – with groupies after concerts – but let's not go into that. It's enough to say that their polaroid collection matches Gene Simmons'. Carl Canedy (drums/vocals), Dave 'Rock' Feinstein (guitar/vocals) and Gary Bordonaro (bass/vocals) make up this 3-piece from Rochester, New York, and have pushed out four exciting albums so far – *The Rods* (1982), *Wild Dogs* (1982), *In The Raw* (1983), and *The Rods Live* (1984).

ROUGH CUTT are another glamorous "are-they-boys-or-girls?" Glam-rock band from LA. They're recording their first album and have already paid their dues by supporting a host of major HM acts in the States. They're also managed by Ronnie Dio's wife, Wendy.

SAGA are the acceptable face of Canadian pomp-rock and a top 30 band in the USA. They're sophisticated, stylish and keyboard-dominated, but that's not to say that they can't rock. They put out their first album on their own label and sold 10,000 export copies to Germany alone. With their seventh album, *Heads Or Tales* (1983) they've finally become big worldwide.

SANTERS are another Canadian band, but this time a 3-man outfit in the Rush vein. Brothers Rick and Mark Santers and Rick Lazaroff do admit to Rush/Triumph influences (Rick Emmett produces them) and have an over-dubbed keyboard sound on their albums which adds to their tight bass-guitar-drums sound. *Metal On Metal* was their first album, with its tribute to Bon Scott of AC/DC, 'Shot Down In Flames', though *Guitar Alley* (1984) is a more impressive platter.

THOR is an out-and-out over-the-top comic book hero who was once Mr Canada. He can bend 2″ thick metal bars, can blow-up hot water bottles (so that they explode) and has a backing group called Mongol Horde. This mild-mannered Canadian is also an excellent pure-Heavy Metal merchant, producing powerful, sharp-edged riff-based metal. He put out a mini-album, *Unchained*, in 1983, and a full album, *Keep The Dogs Away* in 1984.

TORONTO come from Toronto, of course. They're a sextet formed in 1980 and have the distinction of having a female vocalist and a female lead guitarist. It's a distinction that has had them all too often compared to Heart, but Sheron Alton (lead guitar) and Holly Woods (vocals) produce a harder sound. Their first album, *Lookin' For Trouble* went gold in Canada with 170,000 sales, and three albums have followed, including *Girls Night Out* (1984), but they've yet to make a huge impact in the States or Europe.

The last group mentioned here in this North American round-up is the outrageous quartet, **W.A.S.P.** from LA, fronted by sex-maniac Blackie Lawless (bass and vocals). Their first single, 'Animal (I Fuck Like A Beast)' has been banned most places both for its lyrical content and for its sleeve. They're Glam-Metal (of course) and theatrical to the point of absurdity, but they *can* play. Lawless, you may remember, was a New York Doll. Ah . . .

Montrose

If America can be said to have a Heavy Metal triad of groups who have influenced heavy music Stateside the way Purple, Sabbath and Zeppelin did in Britain, then it would be composed of Grand Funk, Kiss and Montrose. And while Montrose made four albums in their relatively brief history, it is for their stunning debut that the band deserves to be remembered.

The band bears the name of Ronnie Montrose, a young American guitarist who got his first break when he was doing some carpentry jobs for Filmore-owner, Bill Graham's partner. After a brief spell as a session guitarist with artists like Van Morrison (it's his excellent acoustic work on *Tupelo Honey*), the Beau Brummels and Gary Wright, Montrose found himself in the Edgar Winter Group, before getting his own band together in late '73 (after turning down the chance of becoming Mott The Hoople's lead guitarist). The three musicians he chose to be in the band were relative unknowns:- Denny Carmassi

on drums, Bill Church on bass and a young physical fitness fanatic, Sammy Hagar, on vocals (yes, *only* vocals!). It was this line-up that cut the first Montrose album in 1973.

Montrose didn't have as great an immediate impact as it should have had, yet years later it is universally recognised as one of the seminal Heavy Metal masterpieces, with no less than four HM classic tracks on it – 'Space Station No. 5', 'Bad Motor Scooter', 'Rock Candy' and 'Rock The Nation'. Unsurprisingly, Montrose found it difficult to live up to their debut, and whilst *Paper Money*, their 1974 album, wasn't bad and had some good music on it (The Dreamer' for instance), it was by no means as impressive. Church had been replaced by Alan Fitzgerald on bass, and when Sammy Hagar left to pursue a solo career, things really began to degenerate. Bob James came in on vocals and sang on the 1975 album, *Warner Brothers Presents Montrose*. Jim Alcivar had been added on keyboards and Randy Hobbs had become the band's bassist, but Ronnie

Montrose had grown rather dissatisfied with the way things were shaping up, and shortly after the fourth album, *Jump On It* appeared in 1976 he finally disbanded Montrose.

Two years later Ronnie Montrose was back, this time with a solo project, *Open Fire*, and a back-up team which had Rick Schlosser on drums, Alan Fitzgerald on bass, Jim Alcivar on keyboards and synthesizers, and – in one of those delightful ironies that rock is full of – Edgar Winter on keyboards. It was a first class rock album, imaginative and melodic, and a perfect showcase for Ronnie Montrose's lyrical guitar style. Compared to the old rocket-powered stuff, however, it was lacking in energy. Sammy Hagar was the inheritor of *that* – or so it seemed in 1978!

Since 1978 Ronnie Montrose has pursued several projects, foremost amongst them the group venture, Gamma, who released three albums. But the man is still living in the shadow of one of the biggest Heavy Metal records of the 70s. Then again, there's some who'd love to achieve that much!

Albums:
Montrose (1973) *Paper Money* (1974) *Warner Brothers Presents Montrose* (1975) *Jump On It* (1976)

Ronnie Montrose:
Open Fire (1978)

Gary Moore

Belfast born Moore has been playing guitar most of his life, but it's only recently that he has received full credit for his exceptional abilities. Gary picked up the guitar at the tender age of eleven, and by the time he was sixteen was in a Belfast group called Skid Row, alongside Phil Lynott (who left shortly afterwards to form Thin Lizzy), staying with them for three years and cutting two albums, *Skid Row* (1970) and *Thirty Four Hours* (1971). He left the band to form his own Gary Moore band, who cut one rather ordinary album in 1973, *Grinding Stone*, then split when Moore was offered the guitarist's job in Thin Lizzy, replacing Eric Bell. But his stay with Lizzy was very short-lived, and lasted only from January to April 1974. When Thin Lizzy brought in twin guitarists Scott Gorham and Brian Robertson, Moore found himself joining Jon Hiseman's Colosseum II, alongside bassist Neil Murray and keyboards man Don Airey.

Moore's stay with Colosseum II lasted from May 1975 to August 1978, in which time they cut three albums, *Strange New Flesh* (1976), *Electric Savage* (1977), and *War Dance* (1977), Moore taking on the role of vocalist on the last two. At the same time he managed to fit in a second session with Thin Lizzy, touring with the band between January and May 1977 (helping out while Brian Robertson was hurt). Phil Lynott obviously liked Moore's guitar style, for when Robertson left to join Wild Horses, Moore was back in Thin Lizzy, this time as a full member of the band. Lizzy were at the height of their popularity in the UK, and Moore cut the *Black Rose* album with them, which went to No. 2 in the British charts. At the same time he took Phil Lynott and Brian Downey, drummer with Lizzy, into the studios with him to cut his first solo album, the superb *Back On The Streets*, with its hit single. 'Parisienne Walkways' (No. 8 in the UK singles chart). It seemed that Gary Moore had, at long last, broken through.

G-Force was Moore's second attempt at leading his own band and proved something of a short-lived failure. An album was cut (but not properly finished) for Jet Records, *Dirty Fingers* (finally released in Japan in 1983, along with a live album, to cash in on Moore's success there), but it was rather a poor affair. Moore disbanded G-Force and worked with Greg Lake on his first solo album, touring the States with Lake's band (Moore is also on Lake's second solo album, *Manoeuvres*). But he still itched to have his own line-up, playing his own songs, and finally achieved that aim in 1982, when he brought in ex-Colosseum II team-mates Murray and Airey, together with Ian Paice on drums and John Sloman on vocals. It was this line-up which cut the *Corridors Of Power* album, released in 1982.

In 1983 Sloman and Airey left, and ex-UFO keyboards man and guitarist Neil Carter joined the band for its tour of

PHOTO SUPPLIED BY IO

the States, supporting Def Leppard. Then, while recording the *Victims Of The Future* album, the band underwent further personnel changes. Neil Murray returned to Whitesnake, and both Bob Daisley and Mo Foster were called in on bass for the sessions before Moore decided on Craig Gruber (ex-Rainbow) as Murray's permanent replacement. When *Victims* was released in January 1984 it went to No. 12 in the UK charts.

When Ian Paice announced that he was leaving the band, Moore brought in Bobby Chouinard on drums to complete his line-up, planning to record a live album for release late in 1984.

For most of his career Moore has been better appreciated for his guitar virtuosity and songwriting ability by his fellow musicians than by the fans, but now that is changing and Moore's talents are at last being recognised in solid sales. It's about time.

Albums:

Grinding Stone (1973) *Back On The Streets* (1978) *Rockin' Every Night – Gary Moore Live In Japan* (Japan, 1981) *Corridors Of Power* (1982) *Dirty Fingers* (Japan, 1983) *Live At The Marquee* (Japan, 1983) *Victims Of The Future* (1984)

Motley Crue

Los Angeles was a pretty jaded city back in 1981 when Motley Crue got together. There were bands – there are always bands in LA! – but no one with any real distinction. The glamorous Crue, too flashy and glittering for words, didn't seem to fit the 'image' of the times. Yet three years on it could well be said that Motley Crue *are* the West Coast image of the moment, with their neo-punk long hairstyles, the tight leather pants and chrome accessories, their chains and spikes. Not only that, but their love of booze, sex and fighting is already notorious – they're young hellraisers in the classic mould.

But image ain't everything – there have been bands in the past with the right look and a lot of hype who have caught the public eye . . . for a time. Motley Crue can't be classed with them. For one thing, their first album, the self-produced "demo", *Too Fast For Love*, released on "Leathur" Records at the beginning of 1982 had sold all its 20,000 copies by the end of May. That's something you can't ascribe to simple image. And if you need any more convincing, then just listen to Mick Mars' guitar solo on 'Knock 'em Dead, Kid' on their 1983 album, *Shout At The Devil*, or the fast-paced tightness of 'Red Hot' on the same album. They aren't poseurs – well, perhaps they *are*, but they aren't *just* poseurs. They can spit in your eye musically, too!

Motley Crue were formed back in February 1981 when bassist Nikki Sixx (now 24) met up with drummer Tommy Lee (23) and decided to join forces. They recruited guitarist Mick Mars (26) and vocalist Vince Neil (23 and the white-haired member of the band!). Liking the look of each other and sharing the same musical tastes they hit it off at once. Surrounded by short-haired new-wave bands, everyone told them they were out of touch. Three years on they're the biggest thing on the West Coast, and fans riot when they make guest appearances at record stores.

Crue come out of the same LA stable as W.A.S.P. and Ratt, but they're the trend-setters, not camp followers (accusations that they're simply copying the New York Dolls are also ridiculous – the music bears it out!). In early 1983 they opened for Kiss and then went on to sell-out the 3500-seater Santa Monica Civic Auditorium three nights running. Early 1984 saw them touring the States on the same bill as Ozzy Osbourne, and August-September sees them touring Europe and playing the huge Castle Donnington festival, supporting AC/DC and Van Halen. A third album is in the offing (if the band can stay out of jail long enough!) and is already anticipated as the one which will break Motley Crue worldwide. *Shout At The Devil* was a top 50 album in the USA last year and has subsequently earned a platinum disc for a million sales. It's almost certain that with their ever-growing following, their colourful look and lifestyle, and, most important of all, their hard-driving, melodic and tight music, Motley Crue will be one of *the* Heavy Metal bands of 1985. That is, if they haven't already become that by the end of 1984.

Albums:
Too Fast For Love (1982)   *Shout At The Devil* (1983)

PHOTO: BARRY LEVINE 1983

Motorhead

Live they're near-lethal, playing at a reputed 126 decidels through a PA system totalling 110,000 Watts. By self-admission they're crass, crude, dirty and rude (see the sleeve inset to *Another Perfect Day* for their tongue-in-cheek self-image), while their name, Motorhead, is American slang for a "speed-freak", those fast-living, amphetamine-popping products of the hippie culture.

Talking of speed-freaks, the Motorhead story began in Canada in 1975 when Lemmy Kilminster, bassist for the acid-head rock group Hawkwind, was arrested for possession of amphetamines. Nothing peculiar in that, you might think, but, to his surprise, Lemmy found himself on a plane home, kicked out after three and a half years in the band. Back in England, Lemmy set about looking for a couple of musicians who wanted to play hard, fast and heavy rock with no frills and tons of energy – the sort of music that would make lawns die. He had a name for the group, and a song, 'Motorhead', written for Hawkwind and released as the B-side to their 1975 single, 'Kings Of Speed'.

The first line-up of Motorhead, which made its debut at the London Roundhouse in July 1975, had Lucas Fox on drums and Larry Wallis (ex-Pink Fairies) on guitar. Their act was under-rehearsed and rather basic. Nonetheless, it was impressive: it had power. A small UK tour followed before, in October, they were asked to support Blue Oyster Cult at London's Hammersmith Odeon. They sounded awful and the music press crucified them. Then, in the winter of 75/76, Motorhead recorded their first album,

bringing in Phil ("Philthy") Taylor on drums halfway through the sessions. Their record company, United Artists, refused to release the tapes of the album, however, releasing them only in 1979 – as *On Parole* – when the group was a big success. But, for the time being, Motorhead seemed still-born.

Ignoring all contracts and protocol, Lemmy set about looking for a second guitarist while negotiating with Stiff Records to record a single. The first was partly achieved when "Fast" Eddie Clarke joined the band. But with Clarke in, Larry Wallis decided he was out. The Stiff single, likewise, *was* recorded ('White Line Fever'), but not released until 1977, because UA slapped on an injunction.

Things changed very little for the band until June 1977 when, free from UA, the band went into the studios to record a single for Chiswick Records. In the two days allocated for the single the band laid down all the backing tracks for an album, *Motorhead*. Chiswick liked it and released it in August 1977. But problems still plagued the band – this time management problems – and they lost their deal with Chiswick. A new manager brought them a new label, Bronze, and things at last began to run smoothly. The band toured constantly, establishing a fanatical following (an album of their live performances from this time, 1978, was released in 1983 as *What's Words Worth*) but it was with the two studio albums, *Overkill* and *Bomber*, both released in 1979, that the band was launched as a major act in the UK. *Bomber* went to

No. 12 in the UK album charts and gained a silver disc, while for the "Bomber" tour in November/December that year, Motorhead introduced their unique lighting rig based on the design of a Heinkel III bomber.

In April 1980 a live EP, 'The Golden Years' went to No. 8 in the UK singles chart. As yet, however, the band were unknown outside their own country, and it was only with the release of the *Ace Of Spades* album in October 1980 that Motorhead were available on vinyl to Heavy Metal fans in the States.

The beginning of 1981 saw Motorhead as one of Britain's leading Heavy Metal acts, a position confirmed by the reception of 'Please Don't Touch' (recorded with the all-girl HM band, Girlschool) which went to No. 5 in the UK singles chart. Then, between April and June, they toured the States for the first time, supporting Ozzy Osbourne's Blizzard Of Oz. They returned to find their live album, the classic *No Sleep 'Til Hammersmith*, released that month, at No. 1 in the UK charts, and when they played the Heavy Metal Holocaust festival at Port Vale, England, in August, they were headliners – supported by Blizzard of Oz amongst others – in front of 40,000 fans.

In 1982 Eddie Clarke left to form his own band, Fastway, and was replaced by Brian "Robbo" Robertson (ex-Wild Horses) for the albums *Iron Fist* and *Another Perfect Day*. But while Motorhead seemed as popular as ever, Robertson's influence on the band's music, making it subtler and softer to achieve some critical credibility, was, as Lemmy later admitted, a backward step for the band. The albums lacked the driving power of the earlier efforts. Robertson left the band in late 1983 and, surprisingly, was followed by Phil Taylor in early 1984 (both joining Thin Lizzy's Phil Lynott for a new project). For Lemmy it was back to 1975. He had a name, a clear idea of the kind of music he wanted to play and was looking for musicians who wanted to play that same kind of old-style crash-and-thrash Motorhead music. That new band played its first gig at the Hammersmith Odeon in May 1984. Ex-Saxon drummer Pete Gill joined Lemmy, along with Phil Campbell and the oddly-named Wurzel, who shared lead guitar duties. The concert was an overwhelming success, hailed by the media and loved by the fans. "Motorhead are BACK" was the word. Bigger, brasher, more enthusiastic, nastier and LOUDER than ever!

Albums:

Motorhead (1977) *Overkill* (1979) *Bomber* (1979) *On Parole* (1979) *Ace Of Spades* (1980) *No Sleep 'Til Hammersmith* (1981) *Iron Fist* (1982) *What's Words Worth* (1983) *Another Perfect Day* (1983) *No Remorse* (1984)*

* Compilation, including 4 new tracks.

The New Wave Of British Heavy Metal

Back in 1979-80, when hard rock music was said by the music critics to be dead and punk was becoming highly formularised and (let's face it) dull, Heavy Metal had its own 'New Wave' movement which was to prove the critics wrong.

This resurgence of Heavy Metal began in England and spread throughout the World, spearheaded by groups like Iron Maiden, Judas Priest, Def Leppard and Saxon. It was a music that had all the energy of punk, yet also produced good songs, virtuosi guitarists and thoughtful stage sets. Black leather and studs were optional, as were mentions of black magic and the occult in the lyrics. Sabbath were the old gods, bring on the new! And so it went on, growing and growing until eventually bands like Def Leppard were bigger than even new wave darlings The Police in the States, their *Pyromania* album kept from the top only by Michael Jackson's *Thriller*.

But apart from the big bands, what else has been happening on the British front since 1979? Who are the bands who've come up on the crest of this new wave? This alphabetical guide, which strays beyond the strict leather-and-studs-riff-heavy merchants, gives an indication of some of the better names on the new British HM circuit.

ALASKA are Bernie Marsden's band. Since leaving Whitesnake, lead guitarist and songwriter Marsden spent a considerable time looking for the right people for a good new band, and has eventually found them. The resultant five-piece have made a good debut in *Heart Of The Storm* (1984).

First Born (1984) is the melodious hard rocking debut of Bradford quintet **BABY TUCKOO**. It's a blockbusting start for the band who have previously impressed with their no-nonsense attitude to music on the club circuit. Rob Armitage is their vocalist and he fronts a band who can really deliver the goods.

BRONZ are a hard rock band with pop undertones. They're an arrogant young five-piece fronted by vocalist Max Bacon, but they can afford a bit of arrogance, being a fine driving HM group whose first album, *Taken By Storm* shows good promise.

DEMON were formed early in 1980 and have produced several highly orthodox Heavy Metal albums, including 1982's *The Unexpected Guest* (Satan? Death?). They're a five-piece from the Midlands with twin guitars and Dave Hill on vocals.

DIAMOND HEAD were the golden boys of 1982, but never quite fulfilled their promise. They were formed in 1977 in Stourbridge in the West Midlands and pushed out their first album on their own independent label. After recording their hard rocking album *Canterbury* they're now without a label again, which is a shame, because this four-piece can live up to its name with tight, crisp-edged metal.

DUMPY'S RUSTY NUTS were formed in 1981 by lead guitarist Dumpy Dunnell and for some while were just a club band in South London, playing their R & B, blues-based hard rock. Their debut album, the double live offering, *Somewhere In England* (1984) moves them up a league and makes them contenders for the hard rock throne.

FASTWAY were formed by ex-Motorhead guitarist, "Fast" Eddie Clark in 1982, bringing in Dave King on vocals, Charlie McCracken on bass and Jerry Shirley on drums. Their second album, *All Fired Up* (1984) shows them to be one of the more original and interesting heavy bands.

GIRLSCHOOL are an all-girl band formed in 1978 by Kim McAuliffe (rhythm guitar and vocals). They've produced four albums so far, *Demolition* (1980), *Hit And Run* (1981), *Screaming Blue Murder* (1982) and *Play Dirty* (1983), but have never quite graduated into the big time despite considerable talent and a lot of hard work. Attractive (both in looks and style), lead guitarist Kelly Johnson has only recently quit the band.

GRIM REAPER are a quartet from Worcester, a "Black Metal" band who aren't as grim as their name suggests. They were formed in 1980 and their debut album, *See You In Hell* (1984) is full of powerfully-charged music.

Bristol-based **JAGUAR** were formed in 1979 by Jeff Cox (bass), Chris Lovell (drums), Garry Peppard (guitar) and Bob Reiss (vocals), Reiss left in 1982 and was replaced by Paul Merrill. They're a slick band whose *War Games* (1983) was a respectable debut. And I hear that they're big in Holland.

MARILLION are an odd name to crop up in this company, but these pomp rockers in the ancient Genesis mould (take it as you will!) have a heavy edge to their music. They're a quintet fronted by singer/lyricist Fish and their two albums so far, *Script For A Jester's Tear* (1983) and *Fugazi* (1984) show them to be a major band of the future.

MARSEILLE recorded their debut album, *Marseille* back in 1979 and then temporarily folded for 18 months when their record company collapsed. This slimmed down four-piece have released a new, hard rock offering, *Touch The Night,* in 1984.

At present **NIGHTWING** haven't a vocalist, since Max Bacon left them to join Bronz, but Bacon is featured on both of the albums cut by this (previously) five-piece HM band, *Stand Up And Be Counted* (1983) and *My Kingdom Come* (1984). Now down to a quartet the present line-up is

Kenny Newton (keyboards), Gordon Rowley (bass), Alec Johnson (guitar) and Steve Bartley (drums).

PALLAS, along with Marillion and Twelfth Night, are in the vanguard of a new-new wave movement termed by some 'second generation progressive rock'. Citing Genesis as their major influence, Pallas manage a schizophrenic balance between soft symphonic rock and hard-edged out-and-out melodic metal ('Arrive Alive' from *The Sentinel*, 1984, is a good instance of the latter). Vocalist Euan Lowson was sacked in June '84, but Graeme Murray

(bass), Ronnie Brown (synthesisers), Niall Mathewson (lead guitar) and Derek Forman (drums) carry on this highly promising band from Aberdeen, Scotland, bringing in young Glaswegian vocalist Alan Reed. Their first album was produced by veteran Yes-producer Eddie Offord.

RAGE are a Liverpool band who cut their first three albums as Nutz between 1977 and 1979. Then, reforming as Rage, they went on to produce a further three albums, *Out Of Control* (1981), *Nice'N'Dirty* (1982) and *Run For The Night* (1983). They're a high energy head-bangers'

group all right, a five-piece with two guitars and a strong, raucous vocalist in Dave Lloyd.

It's always been a mystery why **SAMSON** remained in the second division of Heavy Metal bands. Now that they've split up (May '84) it may well be that their planned live farewell album may break them. Who knows . . . such ironies sometimes happen. Meanwhile, their final studio album, *Don't Get Mad, Get Even* (1984) shows Samson to have developed considerably, with guitarist Paul Samson in excellent form. Mainstream Heavy Metal they may be, but it takes bands like Samson to define Heavy Metal as a form of music.

SHY are from Birmingham, a five-man Journey-style pomp-rock band with a lot of class. Their album, *Once Bitten . . . Twice Shy* (1984) shows influences of Slade and Sweet, but they've a long way to go yet (they're only 19-20 year olds!).

When Tracey Lamb, bassist for Rock Goddess, left to form her own band she stuck with her own sex and put together a group called **SHE**. This four-piece is *very* new and has yet to record its first album, but concert reviews show them to be improving all the time, with Michelle Drees on drums, Chris Bonacci on guitar and Jackie Bochinead on vocals. They're one to watch in the future.

SPIDER are a boogie band. Have no doubts about that. In looks as in sound they come closest to Status Quo (with a touch of Slade thrown in for fun) and have one of the most fanatical fan clubs in the world. Their debut album in 1982 didn't do them justice, but *Rock'N'Roll Gypsies* was followed up by the much better *Rough Justice* in 1984. A Liverpool four-piece, they've toured the British Isles con-

stantly for the last five years with their exciting brand of heads-down-no-nonsense-mindless-boogie.

Reading (as anyone who's been there knows) isn't exactly the centre of the Universe but it has spawned one of the more interesting new wave bands in **TWELFTH NIGHT**. In the Marillion/Pallas stable of progressive rock bands, they're the best of them all, as their *Live And Let Live* (1984) album, recorded live at London's Marquee, proves. They were originally a four-piece instrumental group, influenced by Genesis, before vocalist/lyricist Geoff Mann, joined at the Reading Festival in 1981 (he left the group in October '83, subsequently replaced by Andy Sears). All in all this heavy but intelligent band have produced six albums, most of them self-produced and sold from band-leader Brian Devoli's house. *Fact And Fiction* was their first major studio album in early 1983. I confidently predict huge success for them.

TYGERS OF PAN TANG eventually developed into a really good Heavy Metal band, though no one would have predicted that from their first two albums. The band was formed in late 1978 in Whitley Bay and graduated from a four-piece to a quintet when lead guitarist John Sykes (of Thin Lizzy fame) was drafted in in 1980. *The Cage* is probably their best album, though their retrospective album, *The Best Of . . .* , released in 1984, is a good showcase of their development.

The next three bands deserve to be grouped together under a separate 'Black Metal' heading, because Venom, Witchfinder General and Witchfynde all follow the same basic pattern.

VENOM are a trio from Newcastle, sporting the highly

unlikely names of Mantas (guitar), Cronos (bass/vocals) and Abbadon (drums). They're famous for using massive amounts of explosive materials in their stage act. Venom are black magic fanatics and are as subtle as a sledge-hammer, yet they are noise merchants without equal. Three albums have appeared from them so far, *Welcome To Hell*(1982), *Black Metal*(1983) and *At War With Satan* (1983). They're just plain nasty!

WITCHFINDER GENERAL are, sad to say, a step down from Venom in achievement. *Death Penalty* (1982) and *Friends Of Hell* (1983) never quite lived up to expectations, and this four-piece are still best seen live.

WITCHFYNDE are almost blatant Black Sabbath copyists with heavy occult leanings in their three albums, *Give 'Em Hell* (1980), *Stagefright* (1981) and *Cloak & Dagger* (1983). They're another four-piece whose musical limitations can be estimated at first hearing.

WRATHCHILD are a strange band to end on, because from their image alone one would imagine them to be an LA band into Glam-Metal. But this is Glam-rock UK style, and this four-piece has released one of *the* Heavy Metal albums of 1984 in *Crapp Attakk*, an excellent debut from the band. They're from Worcester (like Grim Reaper) and are heavily into Porn videos and the like. They're certainly one of the dirtiest bands around!

All in all, UK Metal is in good health at present and there seems to be no sign of a further slump in interest. New bands are appearing every month, and by the time this piece appears it's certain to have one or two of the latest upcoming bands missing from its listing. But that's a very healthy sign, after all – one to be welcomed!

Ted Nugent

It's said that in the middle of a Ted Nugent concert – perhaps while the Motor City Madman was playing 'Stormtroopin' or 'Wang Dang Sweet Poon Tang' – a pidgeon flew in front of one of Ted's stacks and dropped dead. Whether it's true or not, it makes a point about Nugent's music and emphasises his maxim, "If it's too loud, you're too old!"

Nugent is one of Heavy Metal's true primitives, as intense and energetic as a caveman on speed (though Nugent is strongly anti-drugs and has thrown players out of his band for indulging), yet he's also as lyrical a guitarist as any you'll come across (listen to 'Together' on *Free-For-All*). On stage he lives up to his nickname, being as maniac a performer as any as he launches into his Scream Dream routine, yet Nugent is a thorough-going professional, managing his own complex affairs and taking enough time off from his music to spend every winter indulging his favourite pastime – hunting in the woods!

Ted Nugent began playing guitar at six and had two years formal guitar tuition at Detroit's Royal School of Music. Then, and as far as his musical development was concerned more important, he had private lessons from one Joe Podorsek, who taught him the basics of R & B and rock 'n' roll. By the time he was ten he was in his first group, the Royal High Boys, and was already obsessed with becoming a rock 'n' roll guitar hero. At thirteen he was in a local band called the Lourds who actually played a 12000-seater hall as support to both the Supremes and the Beau Brummells.

Son of an army Staff Sergeant, Nugent was born in Detroit on 13 December, 1948. At sixteen his parents moved to Chicago, taking a highly indignant Ted with them. The Lourds were forced to split, on the verge of getting a recording contract. Nugent, more determined than ever to become a guitar hero, formed the American Amboy Dukes in 1965, aged sixteen. Then, when he'd graduated, he left home, returned to Detroit, and changed the line-up of the Amboy Dukes. Mainstream offered the band a recording contract.

The band released its debut album, *Amboy Dukes*, in 1967, and the single from the album, the standard R & B number, 'Baby Please Don't Go', was a minor hit. But a year later saw the Dukes go to No. 16 in the National charts with the title track from their second album, *Journey To The Center Of The Mind*. The Amboy Dukes were a six-piece with Rusty Day on vocals, Steve Farmer on rhythm guitar, Rick Lober (and, at another time, Andy Solomon) on keyboards, Greg Arama on bass and Dave Palmer on

drums. Ted Nugent was the star, though, mesmerising audiences with his lightening-fast, hammer-down style of guitar playing and his over-the-top Motor City Madman stage antics. Apart from having a million-selling single, one of the highlights of Nugent's time with the Dukes was their 1968/69 tour, supporting Jimi Hendrix and on occasions opening for Cream.

Hendrix is Nugent's all-time hero, along with the Rolling Stones, with whom he shares a high-energy approach to rock 'n' roll. For Nugent the rock business is a living fantasy, and he's one of rock's great larger-than-life characters; self-sufficient (he kills all his own food), unabashedly chauvinistic (listen to the lyrics on songs like 'My Love Is Like A Tyre Iron'), and self-admittedly reactionary (he's a supporter of the National Rifle Association). But amidst this welter of self-publicity it should not be forgotten that Nugent is one of the finest guitarists in rock: "If God played rock guitar," Nugent claims, "he'd come a poor second to me." An unique guitarist, too, for between 1964 and 1981 he used only one guitar, a semi-acoustic Gibson Byrdland which is usually played by jazz musicians with a soft touch. It feeds back very easily and can prove uncontrollable at even moderate volumes. Nugent's mastery of the instrument has made his style of playing distinctive. In 1981 he experimented with a Les Paul Sunburst, but now he's back to another semi-acoustic Gibson, this time a smaller Fusion. His speed, dexterity and amazing lightness of touch produce a mesmerising wash of heavy sound.

The Amboy Dukes stayed with Mainstream for three albums, then went to Polydor, where a further two albums came out. At this time the Dukes were constantly touring, racking up something like 150 gigs a year. But the formula was beginning to grow jaded, and after another two albums with Discreet, Nugent disbanded the Dukes and went solo, releasing his first album, *Ted Nugent*, in 1975.

Nugent had changed the format of the Dukes several times and with the move from Mainstream had renamed them Ted Nugent And The Amboy Dukes, but from *Ted Nugent* onwards he was to use what were essentially session musicians to back him both live and in the studio. He wrote most of the material and ensured that the guitar sound was dominant in the mix. It was a formula which was instantly successful: *Ted Nugent* went platinum, and the follow-up album, *Free-For-All*, released in 1976, did just as well. *Free-For-All* featured a little-known singer called Meatloaf, as well as Cliff Davies (drums), Rob Grange (bass) and Derek St. Holmes (rhythm).

The late seventies were good years for Nugent. Every album went platinum, and his double live album, *Double Live Gonzo* sold nearly two million copies worldwide. But again the formula was beginning to pall, and the albums *Scream Dream* and *Intensities In Ten Cities* (note the pun?) failed to bring Nugent platinum sales. Personal events may have played some part in this as his wife, Sandra (who had married him at 19) divorced Nugent in 1978. Even so, by 1981 his first eight solo albums had sold in excess of nine million copies worldwide.

1982 saw the release of what was, perhaps, the first disappointing Ted Nugent solo album, *Nugent,* and for a time there was speculation that the Wild Man of Rock 'n' Roll was past it. Perhaps the change of guitars has something to do with it, but the old hammer-down sparkle of the great Gonzo-king wasn't there any more. The fans held their collective breaths for two years, waiting to see if the new album would see Nugent back on form, and when it arrived they breathed out (heavily, of course) with relief. *Penetrator* was crisper, harder and finer than any album since *Cat Scratch Fever,* and more melodic than anything Nugent had ever attempted.

Even so, Ted Nugent must be seen live if you're really going to understand his appeal. Deaf in his left ear, his mammoth stacks now set at waist-height so that he keeps the hearing in his right, Nugent leaps about like an electronic tarzan, bare-chested and screaming-mad, while out front the fans by the PA stacks are suffering sonic abuse. In the meantime there's his 1984 single, 'Tied Up In Love', a blockbuster in the old style. Hard, driving, guitar virtuoso rock 'n' roll music, with few frills.

Albums:
The Amboy Dukes
Amboy Dukes (1967) *Journey To The Center Of The Mind* (1968) *Migration* (1969)

Ted Nugent And The Amboy Dukes
Marriage On The Rocks (1970) *Survival Of The Fittest* (1971) *Journey & Migrations* (1972)★ *Dr. Slingshot* (1972)★ *Ted Nugent And The Amboy Dukes* (1973)★ *Call Of The Wild* (1973) *Tooth, Fang & Claw* (1974)

Ted Nugent
Ted Nugent (1975) *Free-For-All* (1976) *Cat Scratch Fever* (1977) *Double Live Gonzo* (1978) *Weekend Warriors* (1978) *State Of Shock* (1979) *Scream Dream* (1980) *Intensities In Ten Cities* (1981) *The Best Of Ted Nugent Great Gonzos* (1982)★ *Nugent* (1982) *Penetrator* (1984)

★ Compilation albums.

Ozzy Osbourne

You have to admit that the man's slightly crazy. At an American Record Company reception in 1981, he bit the head off a dove. Then, at a concert in Des Moines, early in '82, he tried to bite the head off a bat that a fan had thrown on stage. The half-chewed bat bit back – and Ozzy was rushed to hospital for rabies injections, later on collapsing on stage in Illinois.

Ozzy Osbourne, one time vocalist for Black Sabbath and now leader of his own band, Ozzy Osbourne's Blizzard of Ozz, was born in Aston, Birmingham, in the heart of England's industrial Midlands, on December 3rd 1948. At the age of 13 he says he was a semi-professional burglar. Two months spent in Winson Green Prison on a Grand Larceny charge in 1967 cured him of that activity. He worked for a while in a slaughterhouse (thereby cultivating his notorious sensitivity towards animals!) and began to channel his energies elsewhere, tattooed his kneecaps, and joined what was later to become Black Sabbath, one of rock music's biggest-selling groups.

Towards the end of his stay with Sabbath Osbourne claims he was taking acid and getting drunk most days over a period of two years, and at the end of this time he was almost insane. The sweet leaf has never entirely been dropped – try imagining Ozzy Osbourne as a puritan! –

but he eased off after he shot all seventeen of his cats one night. Such antics not only unified America's moral 'majority' against him but got in the way of the music. Osbourne's last two albums with Black Sabbath, *Technical Ecstasy* and *Never Say Die*, both lacked the sparkle of earlier albums. The old hard, driving music the Sabbath crew were famous for had been diluted in Ozzy's eyes, and he had left the band briefly during the winter of 1977/78. For a while he toyed with the idea of forming a band with guitarist Gary Moore and ex-Deep Purple bassist Glen Hughes, but nothing came of it. Then, when he finally left Black Sabbath for good in 1979, he began looking round for a band who would play the kind of music he felt Sabbath had lost touch with. Osbourne expected Sabbath to split when he left, but they carried on, much to his chagrin. The music press prophesised Osbourne's rapid descent into obscurity, yet in July 1980 he was back, signed up with Jet Records, with an album prepared and a backing group, Blizzard Of Ozz, who began their first tour of the UK in September 1980.

Osbourne's choice for guitarist was Randy Rhoads, whose work with Quiet Riot had impressed him, while on bass was ex-Rainbow man Bob Daisley. Lee Kerslake, Uriah Heep's old drummer, made up the numbers, this line-up recording *Blizzard Of Ozz*, Osbourne's first solo statement. It was an impressive, aggressive debut, released late in 1980, and by early 1981 it was high in the charts both sides of the Atlantic. It wasn't long before the album went gold in the States and the band was touring over there to rapturous applause from packed audiences. But it was a slightly different band that made the first US tour in May 1981; Kerslake and Daisley were out, and Rudy Sarzo (bass) and Tommy Aldridge (ex Pat Travers/Gary Moore drummer) were in. With this line-up Osbourne recorded his second album, *Diary Of A Madman*, and played the Heavy Metal Holocaust at Stoke-On-Trent in August 1981 (as headliners, after Black Sabbath had pulled out!). It was a good year for Osbourne, for *Diary* went gold shortly after its release, while *Blizzard Of Ozz* had eventually chalked up sufficient sales in the States to earn itself a platinum disc. Within his first year Osbourne had done all the critics said he wouldn't. He was more popular than ever.

From his earliest days with Black Sabbath Ozzy had been fascinated by the supernatural, and in his stage act there is a great deal of pure theatre, sometimes bordering on melodrama, but always superbly carried off. Make-up and stage sets, death-and-destruction music and blood-curdling lyrics all play their part. As does a midget, whose job it is to throw raw offal into the audience during performances. Recently he had dabbled in mini horror epics for his videos, and live his appearance as a werewolf is quite startling. But there's an element of the old Ozzy in there too, the peace signs given and received, the total rapport with his audience. Indeed, it's true to say that Ozzy Osbourne is a far better live performer than studio technician, though his solo work with Blizzard Of Ozz has maintained a high standard.

During 1982 Bob Daisley returned to Osbourne's backing group, and ex-Rainbow man Don Airey joined on keyboards. But disaster struck the band on March 19th, 1982 while they were touring. Randy Rhoads was in a light plane with several others when, after several mock dive-bombing runs, the plane's wing clipped the truck and crashed, killing all in it. Osbourne decided to carry on with the tour, and flew in ex-Gillan guitarist Bernie Torme. Torme finished the tour and then left. Osbourne's full-time replacement for the much-missed Rhoads was guitarist Jake E. Lee, who had been in the LA band Rough Cutt.

But before Lee joined . . . well, there was something Ozzy Osbourne wanted to get out of his system. 1982 saw Black Sabbath planning to release *Live At Last*, a double album recorded with Ronnie Dio. To Osbourne it was tantamount to an act of sacrilege; he felt it ruined Sabbath. His answer was to play two nights at The Ritz, New York, and release a double album celebrating the occasion – four sides of his favourite Black Sabbath numbers!

Talk Of The Devil, released at the end of 1982, must have delighted the Sabbath fans as well as winning converts to Ozzy Osbourne's solo crusade. Backed up by Tommy Aldridge, Rudi Sarzo (bass) and Brad Gillis (guitar), Osbourne seemed to prove his point – that the impact of songs like 'Black Sabbath', 'The Wizard' and 'Paranoid' (which seems to always close his live set) depended upon his unique vocal style. By January 15th, 1983 the album was No. 14 in the US album charts, where it stayed for another two weeks.

For a brief while in 1983 Osbourne brought in Carmine Appice on drums, but the ex-Vanilla Fudge heavy stayed only until March 1984, when Aldridge returned. Meanwhile, the band had recorded and released *Bark At The Moon* (with Aldridge on drums), Osbourne's best solo effort to date, with the excellent 'Waiting For Darkness' and the delightful werewolf tale, 'Bark At The Moon'. During the filming of the video for 'So Tired', the hit single from the album, Osbourne had an encounter with a broken mirror, and discovered later that he had splinters of glass in his throat. It seems to have done no real harm

PHOTO: REX FEATURES

though, and the band, and Osbourne, have again toured the States, outraging those stern Mid-West moralists – but delighting an ever-growing number of fans.

Albums:
Blizzard Of Ozz (1980) *Diary Of A Madman* (1981)
Talk Of The Devil (1982) *Bark At The Moon* (1983)

Quiet Riot

Quiet Riot emerged triumphantly from the second division of American heavy metal in 1983 with their hit version of the Slade song 'Cum On Feel The Noize'. This was a just reward for a band who had been hard on the gig circuit with ceaseless energy and devotion: in 1983 alone they played 220 dates.

But fame was a long time coming and earlier days even witnessed a tragedy when founder member Randy Rhoads, who had quit the band when their outlook appeared bleak to join forces with Ozzy Osbourne, died in a plane crash.

Essentially a Los Angeles band, Quiet Riot were formed as far back as 1975 when singer Kevin DuBrow met up with guitarist Randy Rhoads, bass player Rudy Sarzo and drummer Frankie Banazi. They soon built up a solid West Coast following with an invigorating set of hard rock tunes played to high decibel levels and with energy to spare. But somehow, they were unable to progress further, and never played outside California. Purveyors of bone-crunching heavy metal very much in the British style, the group took their name from a quote of Status Quo's Rick Parfitt, who once said he'd call his band that if he ever quit Quo. Turned down by all American record labels, the original line-up recorded two albums for the Japanese market, which are now obviously collectors items, but which they now disown. "They're rubbish. Randy hated them", says Kevin DuBrow.

Discouraged by their lack of recognition, the virtuoso Randy departed in 1979 for the Osbourne fold and his sad destiny, while Rudy Sarzo also abandoned the ranks to join rival formation Angel. Kevin and Frankie then decided to change the group's name to DuBrow. Times were difficult; Rudy rejoined briefly before moving, also to Osbourne pastures. Frankie now recalls that in order to make ends meet, he was obliged to do much session work in those days. The band finally caught the attention of producer Spencer Proffer, who signed them to his Pasha Label. He introduced guitar player Carlos Cavazo to the band and the recording of what was to become *Metal Health* began. The initial idea was for both Randy and Rudy to guest on one track, but this was abandoned when Randy died a few weeks later. In the event, Rudy felt more comfortable with his old mates and ended up playing on most of the album's tracks. So the band adopted the Quiet Riot moniker again, in August 1982: "It couldn't be called DuBrow any more. And anyway, it wasn't much of a hook name – Du What?", reflects Kevin.

The album was released in February 1983 and began its slow but inexorable climb up the US charts. Of course, the band helped it along, first with gigs outside California, supporting ZZ Top, Iron Maiden, Loverboy and Black Sabbath, then with adventurous videos, popular on the influential MTV cable channel. In one such video Kevin had to jump 83 feet out of a building, albeit in a parachute harness . . .

In performance, Quiet Riot are a splendid example of a hard rock group with melodious touches, and are very much a people's band. Kevin's unsounded enthusiasm soon proves contagious, as do his clever stage routines with Carlos, always a favourite feature of their punchy act. Their forthcoming album, which they really see as their second, should establish them as an important fixture in the worldwide heavy metal scene – and perhaps prove a second chart-topper for the band.

Albums:

Quiet Riot (1977, Japan) *Quiet Riot II* (1978, Japan)
Metal Health (1983) *Condition Critical* (1984)

PHOTO: LAURIE PALADINO PIX 1982

Rainbow

If there was one group on the heavy rock circuit that was the brainchild of a single man, it was Ritchie Blackmore's Rainbow. Disillusioned with the kind of music Deep Purple were making on the albums *Burn* and *Stormbringer*, Blackmore kept back his own material for a solo project – wanting to make an album of hard rock that wasn't tainted by the blues/soul influences David Coverdale had been introducing into Purple's act. The situation came to a head when Blackmore wanted to record a cover of the Quatermass song, 'Black Sheep Of The Family'. Blackmore went into the studios with another of Purple Records' acts, Elf, who had supported Deep Purple on tour in the States in late 1972. It was late '74, and whilst Blackmore stayed with Deep Purple, his days with the band were numbered.

Ritchie Blackmore was born in Weston-Super-Mare, in Somerset, on April 14th 1945, and by the time he was 16 was in Screaming Lord Sutch's backing group, the Savages, as a professional guitarist. After a spell with the Outlaws and as a session musician, Blackmore joined Deep Purple at the end of 1967. Even then he was one of the most accomplished guitarists in Britain, a thorough professional with seven years experience and a clear cut idea of the kind of music he wanted to play.

Elf were formed from the core of a group called the Electric Elves in the summer of 1970. They were playing the club and bar circuit looking for a record contract when Roger Glover and Ian Paice of Purple spotted them and signed them. There were various shake-ups in their line-up subsequently, but the group which Ritchie Blackmore took into the studios in Munich in early 1975 to record his solo project consisted of Ronnie Dio (vocals), Gary Driscoll (drums), Mickey Lee Soule (keyboards) and Craig Gruber (bass).

Blackmore's impatience with his fellow musicians was already infamous and, before he quit Deep Purple in April 1975, he had been the chief instigator of most of the changes in the band's personnel. This history of change

and change again was to extend into Rainbow. Elf became Ritchie Blackmore's Rainbow in May 1975, having shed their lead guitarist Steve Edwards, releasing *Ritchie Blackmore's Rainbow* in August 1975 (it reached No. 30 in the US charts). As Blackmore's Rainbow, however, this band was never to tour; Blackmore broke up the band in September 1975 and brought in ace session drummer Cozy Powell, bassist Jimmy Bain and keyboards man Tony Carey. Of the first Rainbow line-up, only Ronnie James Dio appeared when the band lined up on stage in Philadelphia for their first gig on 15th November 1975.

Dio's strong voice and Blackmore's distinctive guitar playing were to be the one constant in the band over the next four years, the two men jointly composing all of the material on the second Rainbow album, *Rainbow Rising*, released in July 1976, and most of the Rainbow songs on the next. *Rising* was the first album to do well in the UK, reaching No. 11 in the charts, though in the US Rainbow's star was never to be so bright again. The music, however,

was good hard-edged heavy rock, reminiscent of the Purple of *In Rock* era, yet with tracks like 'Do You Close Your Eyes' suggesting a distinctive Rainbow sound. The band toured extensively and released a double live album, *On Stage*, which got to No. 7 in the UK charts in the summer of 1977. But Blackmore's dissatisfaction with the group's make-up resulted in both Jimmy Bain and Tony Carey being fired in February 1977. Carey was recalled for six months, then fired again. In the interim, bassist Mark Clarke had come and gone, his playing on the sessions for Rainbow's fourth album not up to Blackmore's exacting standards.

In August 1977 yet another new Rainbow line-up was announced, this time introducing keyboards player David Stone (ex-Symphonic Slam) and bassist Bob Daisley (ex-Widowmaker). This group recorded *Long Live Rock 'N' Roll* (released in March 1978) which went to No. 7 in the UK charts. Once again, however, success in the States evaded Rainbow, despite their extensive 1978 tour. In

November Blackmore brought in ex-Purple mate Roger Glover on bass and Don Airey (Cozy Powell's ex-keyboard man in Cozy Powell's Hammer). At last it seemed the band matched Blackmore's conception. But then, in January 1979, Ronnie Dio dropped a bombshell; he was leaving to join Black Sabbath. The band carried on without a vocalist for a time, laying down the music for their next album, then in April 1979 Blackmore recruited ex-Marbles vocalist Graham Bonnet, whose solo album, released in 1977, had impressed Blackmore.

With Bonnet belting out the vocals, the band finished *Down To Earth* in the following few months and released it in the summer of 1979. It was an instant success and spawned two hit singles, the Blackmore/Glover composition, 'All Night Long' (an anthem to groupies if there ever was one!) and 'Since You've Been Gone', an old Russ Ballard number done with Rainbow's new-found zest. It seemed the new line-up would be the one to break through in the States, but neither singles or albums made a great impression, and by the time Rainbow re-entered the studio to cut their next album Cozy Powell and Graham Bonnet had moved on to other fields, with Bobby Rodinelli (drums) and Joe Lynn Turner (vocals) taking their place. *Difficult To Cure*, released in 1981, saw Rainbow maintaining their place as one of the UK's top heavy acts (they had headlined the Castle Donnington Monsters Of Rock festival the previous August – Powell's last performance with the band) but making no inroads in the USA.

Since their 1979 album, *Down To Earth*, Roger Glover had produced the band, and his crisp work on songs like 'I Surrender' (another Russ Ballard number) got the very best out of the music.

Spring 1981 saw Rainbow touring with the Pat Travers Band, promoting their new material; it also saw Don Airey leave the band and David Rosenthal join on keyboards. It was this combination that recorded *Straight Between The Eyes* (released 1982) and their first minor US success came with the single 'Stone Cold', which reached No. 40 in the charts in June 1982. Then, when Bobby Rodinelli left and Chuck Burgi joined on drums, Rainbow achieved its final form, recording *Bent Out Of Shape*, which was released in 1983.

Throughout its years, Rainbow didn't so much develop as perfect Ritchie Blackmore's ideas about heavy rock music. The 1981 compilation album, *The Best Of Rainbow* is a perfect illustration. Without the sleeve notes for a guide it would be difficult to date the songs (which are – deliberately it seems – in no chronological order), and, as a result, Blackmore's intentions with the band become far easier to discern. *In Rock* and *Machine Head*, those classic Deep Purple albums of the early '70s, were his model – the kind of music he wanted to write and play – and when the opportunity came in early 1984 to rejoin his Deep Purple colleagues of that time Blackmore took it. And so Rainbow, Ritchie Blackmore's Rainbow all along, even if he dropped those two possessive words, are deceased.

Until the next time round?

Albums:
Ritchie Blackmore's Rainbow (1975) *Rainbow Rising* (1976) *On Stage* (1977) *Long Live Rock 'N' Roll* (1978) *Down To Earth* (1979) *Difficult To Cure* (1981) *The Best Of Rainbow* (1981)★ *Straight Between The Eyes* (1982) *Bent Out Of Shape* (1983)

★ Compilation album.

Rock Goddess

How many groups can claim to have a nine-year-old drummer? A hard rock drummer at that, who'd rather be beating hell out of the skins than playing with her schoolmates. Well, Rock Goddess, formed in 1977 by sisters Jody and Julie Turner with their friend Tracey Lamb, can claim that much. And if these days drummer Julie is sweet sixteen and a drum veteran of seven years, her early enthusiasm and expertise at the drums (her hero is Roger Taylor of Queen) is still impressive.

Elder sister Jody Turner, born in 1963, is the band's songwriter, lead vocalist and guitarist. And a good guitarist too. Indeed, to view Rock Goddess as just another novelty act, an all-girl heavy rock band, is unfair, because on the showing of their first two albums they deserve to be treated alongside the best of the (usually male) heavy metal acts. Influenced by Zeppelin, AC/DC, Y & T and Iron Maiden, their own music is slowly developing its own distinctive feel. Their rhythm section is very heavy, allowing Jody's solos to come across powerfully, while her vocals are given a harmonic backing by the other two girls.

Looking back, it seems quite natural that the Turner girls should have become rock musicians. Their father ran a music shop in their native Wandsworth and the girls lacked no equipment or opportunity for rehearsal – nor encouragement, for their father was himself a musician in the sixties and is now their manager. They played their first gig at the 101 Club in Clapham (also in South London) in the summer of 1981, followed by a number of gigs about the UK. Their first appearance on disc was on a compilation album by Girlfriend Records, who wanted to put out a showcase of all-female bands, called *Making Waves.* Their contribution was 'Make My Night'. The record companies paid attention, and in 1982 A & M signed them.

Their first album, *Rock Goddess,* appeared early in 1983. It was surprising for its variety, its virtuosity and its professionalism, and numbers like 'Satisfied Then Crucified' demonstrate a heavy-rocking power that was more normally associated with macho, leather-studded males. There was nothing soft or cloying about the album, and it was an instant favourite with heavy metal fans, spawning the moderately successful single, 'My Angel'. The band were further boosted by being invited to tour Europe as support to Def Leppard. But in the interim bassist Tracey Lamb had left to form She, and Dee O'Malley (a "failed guitarist" who had advertised her services as bassist in the Music Papers) met the sisters, clicked, and joined the band. With the new line-up the girls recorded their second album, *Hell Hath No Fury,* the songs penned once again by Jody Turner.

More polished and impressively accomplished, *Hell Hath No Fury* was launched with a tour of the States, supporting their heavy rock heroes, Y & T, while a single, Gary Glitter's 'I Didn't Know I Loved You (Till I Saw You Rock And Roll)' climbed the charts in the UK. Julie had to have a tutor during the Stateside tour, however, to comply with the law. Which is another way of saying, I suppose, that there's so much potential in this band – they're still so young – that it's hard to see them not making it big in the near future. With a new album due at the end of 1984 and more touring underway it seems that nothing is going to stop them.

Albums:
Rock Goddess (1983)   *Hell Hath No Fury* (1983)

Rush

Back in 1969, in Toronto, Canada, three fifteen-year-old schoolboys, Geddy Lee (bass), Alex Lifeson (guitar) and John Rutsey (drums), helped by their sixteen year old manager, Ray Danniels, formed a band, Rush, to play the kind of music they had come to love; heavy, melodic power-rock – the kind Jimi Hendrix, Cream, and the newly-formed Led Zeppelin were playing. By 1971 (when they could legally enter such places!) the band was playing the local bar and club circuit, winning a small following for their idiosyncratic music.

Their first big break came in late 1973, however, when they were chosen to support the New York Dolls when they played Toronto. Rush upstaged the Dolls and realised for the first time that their ambitions were no idle dreams. Danniels raised the money to buy studio time and the band went in to cut their first album, *Rush.*

Making it in the face of record company indifference and media hostility has always been part of Heavy Metal's folklore, but Rush have had more than their fair share of indifference and hostility. *Rush* was ignored by all the major Canadian labels. Danniels, his faith in the band absolute, sold his management agency and set up a label, Moon, on which to release a limited number of Rush's first album. Unpublicised, its word-of-mouth sales were nonetheless sufficient to make the venture a success. Not only that, but one copy found its way south, into the States, and onto the desk of a record executive at Mercury Records. Mercury had heard from their act, the Dolls, how good these unknowns were, and the record proved it. Mercury signed Rush for a two-record deal.

It was 1974 and *Rush,* released by Mercury, had sold 75,000 copies in the USA. An extensive tour of the States had been organised, and then, suddenly, John Rutsey quit through ill health. The band, desperate to find a replacement, held auditions before remembering a local drummer, Neil Peart. Peart was called in, tried out, and given the job. Rush in its modern form was born.

The earlier Rush were a lot heavier than most bands on

the rock circuit, as tracks like 'Working Man' prove, but Peart's influence – mainly as lyricist – changed their musical approach. They had been likened to Led Zeppelin, but with the 1975 albums, *Fly By Night* and *Caress of Steel*, they began to formulate their distinctive sound, mixing heavy riffs with complex time signatures and symphonic effects. People still compared them to Zeppelin, but some critics started noticing a bit of Genesis and Yes thrown in there. Yet it was Rush, pure Rush, and still is. You can think of all manner of comparatives, but none are comprehensive enough – Rush remain quite unique in the Heavy Metal/Progressive Rock field.

Perhaps the most important element Peart added to the band was his fascination, reflected in the songs on his first five studio albums with Rush (and, indeed, on their 1984 single, 'The Body Electric'), with science fiction/fantasy. This reached its height, perhaps, on the 1976 album, *2112*, Rush's equivalent of what right-wing novelist Ayn Rand did in her 1938 novel, *Anthem* (incidentally, a track from *Fly By Night* also bears this title). *2112* is a concept album, depicting a future world run by despotic priests (communists?) to whom logic is law and the individual anathema. But Peart's imaginative venture also brought hostility from certain sectors of the music press, in particular from Britain's rock newspaper, NME, champions of the punk movement, who in February 1978 accused Rush of being crypto-fascists – a label which, unfairly, has stuck in the heads of some of rock's poorer critics ever since.

By 1978, however, Rush were launched as a major international act. A double album of their live performances, *All The World's A Stage*, had appeared in 1976, and the band, headliners in North America, toured Britain in 1977, recording their new album, *A Farewell To Kings*, at Rockfield Studios in Wales. It was their finest album to date, and, on tracks like 'Xanadu', displayed a depth of feeling and wealth of musicianship which was second to none in the rock field. Like the previous two albums it went platinum in Canada and gold in the States. Rush had arrived.

Yet as far as the media were concerned – and in particular the radio stations who determined what was being heard on the airwaves – Rush didn't exist. Their massive sales were based on touring and word-of-mouth alone. To the media they were just another heavy trio – big in Canada, but so what? It was an attitude that changed little even when *Hemispheres* appeared in October 1978, going gold in the States very quickly. The audience for Rush's music was growing all the time, yet because they made no singles the DJs ignored them totally.

It was a situation which could not last. *Permanent Waves*, their January 1980 release, not only spawned a hit single in 'The Spirit of Radio' but went to No. 4 in the US charts and No. 3 in the UK. By this time each of their tours was seen by in excess of a million fans and the group was lugging $600,000 of equipment about the World in four huge trucks. They had become too big to ignore. Without having compromised an inch, without media hype, and in the face of unjust criticism, they had reached the top of their profession.

Permanent Waves had begun a movement away from symphonic-rock and towards shorter, more economical pieces. *Moving Pictures* and, more dramatically, *Signals*, continued this process. Comparatives were no longer possible, except to the tone-deaf. This was pure Rush music; crisp, melodic, driving, and with a delivery which, on tracks like 'Red Barchetta' and 'New World Man' were exhilarating (the latter track getting to No. 21 in the US singles charts in October 1982). Geddy Lee had often been accused of sounding too much like Robert Plant, but his high-pitched vocals on the recent albums are too distinctive and assured to remind you of anything other than the earlier Rush albums.

Unlike many other bands who had made it, Rush continued to tour worldwide, at the same time utilising the new video medium to add a visual dimension to their music (they've done videos of much of their material since 'Xanadu'). A live double of material from their later albums (mixed with a few older numbers) appeared in 1981, *Exit . . . Stage Left*, displaying the range and virtuosity of Rush's music. It spawned another minor hit single in 'Tom Sawyer', the video of which shows Rush at their mesmerising live best, sounding more like a six-piece than a three man outfit.

1984 sees Rush touring North America yet again and with a new album – their first without their 'fourth man', producer Terry Brown – making a strong impact on the charts worldwide. *Grace Under Pressure* is perhaps their, strongest, most sophisticated album yet – a clear progression technically and a further step away from conceptual, symphonic rock (typified by 'The Fountain Of Lamneth' on *Caress Of Steel*) and towards more economic tone-pieces. It is a development which, as on the complex but heavy 'Kid Gloves', can only be applauded.

Albums:

Rush (1974) *Fly By Night* (1975) *Caress Of Steel* (1975) *2112* (1976) *All The World's A Stage* (1976) *A Farewell To Kings* (1977) *Hemispheres* (1978) *Permanent Waves* (1980) *Moving Pictures* (1981) *Exit . . . Stage Left* (1981) *Signals* (1982) *Grace Under Pressure* (1984)

Saxon

Saxon came to prominence during the 1979/80 resurgence of Heavy Metal – the "New Wave of British Heavy Metal" as it came to be known – and became identified in the eyes of the British media as the definitive denim-and-leather, medium-tempo, high-volume band. Which was fair enough, because that, essentially, was what Saxon were about: "red noise", one journalist called their sound, describing such anthemic songs as 'Wheels Of Steel', 'Strong Arm Of The Law' and 'And The Bands Played On'.

The band was formed in 1977, in Barnsley, South Yorkshire, and kept the same line-up until 1981 when original drummer Pete Gill left (later to join Motorhead) and Nigel Glockler joined. Vocalist and spokesman for the band is Biff Byford, while Paul Quinn and Graham Oliver are their two mad axemen, providing their twin guitar sound on tracks like 'Dallas, 1pm' (a song about the assassination of Kennedy). Making up the rhythm section for Saxon is bassist Steve Lawson.

From the first Saxon were determined to follow the traditional British working-class, heavy-metal formula of extensive touring to establish their hard-core following. This proved so successful that after a 1979 tour supporting Motorhead, their 1980 release *Wheels Of Steel* went into the top 5 of the UK charts, and they found themselves on the crest of a wave of new interest in Heavy Metal. *Strong Arm Of The Law*, released only seven months later, met with a similar enthusiastic response from the fans. Encouraged by this reception the band launched a world tour in 1981, returning late in the year to release *Denim And Leather*, which went silver in the UK.

1982 saw Saxon out on the road again, with major tours of the USA and Britain – tours boosted by the release of a live album, *The Eagle Has Landed*, recorded at the end of 1981.

Saxon's brand of "ram-it-down-your-throat" music perhaps reached its height with the 1983 album, *The Power And The Glory*, which climbed to No. 15 in the UK charts

in March that year, while the 1984 album, *Crusader*, marked a slight softening in the music. *Crusader* was more commercial than previous albums, though certainly no less heavy; a maturation more than a compromise with market demands.

In the last two years Saxon have concentrated on touring the States (though not wholly to the exclusion of their British fans, as "The 1984 Crusade" proved), and with a vociferous and loyal following on both sides of the Atlantic the band seem set to shake off that 'typical NWOBHM' label they've been stuck with and at long last be recognised for their own merits.

Albums:

Saxon (1979) *Wheels Of Steel* (1980) *Strong Arm Of The Law* (1980) *Denim And Leather* (1981) *The Eagle Has Landed* (1982) *The Power And The Glory* (1982) *Crusader* (1984)

Michael Schenker

Not all rock 'n' roll bands are as clean-living as those Sheffield tea-suppers, Def Leppard. The road is littered with the casualties of drugs and hard drinking – rock stars who have succumbed to the temptations of the lifestyle, and gone under, through pressure or hedonistic excess. Michael Schenker, perhaps the finest guitarist to come out of Germany (a fact his brother Rudy would probably endorse), almost went under.

Michael Schenker began his professional career in rock in 1971 when, with Rudy, he formed the Scorpions. They made a promising debut album, *Lonesome Crow*, but in June 1973 Michael left them to join UFO, then one of the top acts in Germany. At first it was a temporary arrangement, but Schenker stayed, and recorded his first UFO album with Way, Mogg and Parker, *Phenomenon*, in 1974. When Paul Chapman joined the band as second guitarist, Schenker found himself once again in the same kind of five-piece line-up that the Scorpions had had. It's a line-up Schenker seems to favour, letting the rhythm guitar harmonise and complement his lead playing, or form a melodic background to his searing solos.

In Schenker's time with UFO they climbed out of relative obscurity in the States and the UK and became a major chart act. Schenker appeared on *Force It*, *No Heavy Pettin'*, *Lights Out*, *Obsession* and *Strangers In The Night*, their live double released in 1973, taking the greater share of the solos and helping compose a good proportion of their material. His hard drinking remained a problem, however, and he left UFO in November 1977 for that reason, spending a brief while in hospital. Early in 1979 he returned to the Scorpions, but stayed only a fortnight before deciding to launch a solo venture.

Schenker's first solo album, *The Michael Schenker Group*, was finally completed and released in August 1980, and went to No. 8 in the UK charts. It had been recorded with a number of session musicians, but when Schenker toured with "The Michael Schenker Group" it was a different line-up: Gary Barden (vocals), Cozy Powell (drums), Chris Glen (bass) and Paul Raymond, an ex-UFO colleague (rhythm guitar). Calling themselves MSG, they were received enthusiastically and their first group album, *MSG*, released in September 1981, reached No. 4 in the UK charts. To follow up its success Schenker released a double live album only a few months later, recorded in Japan, at the Budokan, where Schenker was greeted as an old favourite, a star from his UFO days. The album confirmed Schenker's success, getting to No. 5 in the UK charts.

Throughout its early history MSG suffered from Schenker's personal problems. By the beginning of 1982 Raymond was gone, then in February Graham Bonnet (ex-

Rainbow vocalist) joined in place of Barden. Cozy Powell upped and left in April, to be replaced by Ted McKenna. But this new line-up proved incompatible live. Bonnet stayed long enough to sing vocals on *Assault Attack*, then left. Schenker brought Gary Barden back in and carried on, but the new album only reached No. 19 in the UK charts.

In 1983 Schenker drafted in Andy Nye on guitar and MSG recorded their third studio album, *Built To Destroy*, which sold in excess of 100,000 copies in the UK. More important, however, was the news in August that Schenker's hell-raising days were over: he had given up drink and drugs. It heralded a new era for MSG, and in April 1984, with new bassist David Feldman replacing Glen, Schenker and his band toured the States, sometimes supporting Ted Nugent, sometimes headlining their own show. The decline which had paralleled Schenker's own physical decay was halted. The new-look Schenker, hair slicked back and guitar-playing better than ever, won over audiences throughout the States. A new live album, *Rock Will Never Die* (a double in the States, a single in the UK) began climbing the charts on June 1974, proving the Mad Axeman with his Flying-V guitar more popular than ever before.

Albums:
The Michael Schenker Group (1980) *MSG* (1981) *One Night At Budokan* (1981) *Assault Attack* (1982) *Built To Destroy* (1983) *Rock Will Never Die* (1984)

Scorpions

The German rock scene was in full swing, with bands like Can, Tangerine Dream and Amon Duul II receiving attention in the UK, when a small amateur band from Hanover turned professional and recorded their first album, under the guidance of the now-legendary Conny Plank. The band was the Scorpions, and unlike most of their German contemporaries they wanted to play not experimental rock but heavy, American-influenced rock. That first line-up had brothers Rudolf and Michael Schenker as lead guitarists, Klaus Meine on vocals, Wolfgang Dziony on drums and Lothar Heimberg on bass. Their album, *Lonesome Crow* was a minor hit in Germany, and Scorpions launched out on the first of their now customary extensive tours, playing 130 gigs in their homeland. It was their first small taste of success and led to them being asked to write the soundtrack for a movie. *The Cold Paradise.* 1973 saw the release of their debut album worldwide, while on the road the band was supporting groups like Chicken Shack and UFO when they toured Germany. But that tour with UFO almost ended Scorpions rise to fame before it got started, because in June 1973 UFO shed guitarist Bernie Marsden after he'd missed a gig and drafted in Michael Schenker.

Rudolf Schenker broke up the band, but then relented, and, two months later, presented a new line-up, Heimberg and Dziony leaving and Ulrich Roth (guitar), Francis Buchholz (bass) and Jurgen Rosenthal (drums) coming in. This new Scorpions changed record labels, and in early 1974 recorded their second album, *Fly To The Rainbow.* Ulrich Roth's influence was noticeable on the lyrical and lengthy title track with its mixture of acoustic guitar, hard rock and Hendrix-like space-rock. It was an album which again won them much acclaim in their home country, including a "Most Promising New Band" award from German pop magazine *Popfoto.*

At the end of 1974 drummer Rosenthal was replaced by Belgian Rudy Lenners who joined the band for their first gigs outside of Germany in early 1975. Touring as support act to Sweet they played in front of large audiences for the first time; audiences which were to make their 1975 album, *In Trance,* their best-seller yet in their homeland. But the signs were there already that the Scorpions could be big worldwide, and in November 1975 they set out on their first tour of the UK, following it up in 1976 with their first extensive tour of Europe. Meanwhile, Japan, who had embraced UFO with fervour, had made *In Trance* a hit album, and their 1976 album, *Virgin Killer* added to their reputation both at home and in Japan. But the band wanted to break into the UK and US markets – to gain acceptance in those countries where there music was rooted – and in 1977 they toured the UK yet again.

For their 1977 album, *Taken By Force,* drummer Rudy Lenners had quit, owing to ill health, and present drummer Herman Rarebell joined the band. Their popularity was also boosted by the release of two compilation albums that year. They were on the verge of international success. It seemed a good time to follow up the interest that had been shown in their music in Japan.

The 1978 tour of Japan was an eye-opener to the Scorpions. Like UFO in 1971, they were welcomed as super-stars, their five big concerts over there sell-outs, two being recorded for a double live album, *Tokyo Tapes,* released the next year. It was the end of the first phase in their development and, as if recognising this, Ulrich Roth left the band to form his own group, Electric Sun. After auditioning something like 150 guitarists, the Scorpions chose a local guitarist, Matthias Jabs. With Jabs in the band the Scorpions went out on the road again, harder and heavier than ever. The end of 1978 saw them playing a festival before 90,000 fans, then entering the studios to cut the first album of their second phase, *Lovedrive.*

Lovedrive was released in January 1979, and by April was No.36 in the UK charts and No.55 in the US. For a brief period Jabs was out, when Michael Schenker returned after his time in UFO. But Michael didn't stay more than a few weeks, and Jabs was soon back, helping give the band its sharp edge. At long last the band was making headway in the UK and an 11-date tour there was a sell-out, but the big test was their first proper tour of America later that year, when they took their non-stop, all-action roadshow in support of Ted Nugent, playing 20,000 capacity audiences regularly. When they returned in December, supporting Sammy Hagar and Rainbow, they had already established a hard core of Scorpions fans in the States. *Animal Magnetism*, released in April 1980, once more showed increased sales, reaching No.23 in the UK charts, No.52 in the States.

Spring 1981 brought an enforced rest for the band when singer Klaus Meine underwent surgery to remove nodes on his vocal chords. The operation was a success, and later in the year the band returned to the studios to finish the *Blackout* album – their best to date, which won widespread critical acclaim. Better yet, when it was released in April 1982 it scuttled up the charts on both sides of the Atlantic, assisted by the "Blackout" tour which was a sell-out wherever it went, the Scorpions' frenetic stage-style winning them yet more fans. In the UK and the US the album climbed to No.11 in the charts and eventually went platinum in the States, thanks partly to concerts such as the Us Festival, where the Scorpions were second on the bill to Van Halen in front of an estimated 350,000 people.

In twelve years the band had grown more sophisticated,

their stage act more polished, while their studio work was ever more exacting. *Love At First Sting*, released in March 1984, proved not only their best album to date, but also their best-selling; it was their second platinum disc and sold a reputed 15,000 copies a day in the States. But recording the album had its problems. Drummer Rarebell's health failed during the opening sessions (like Michael Schenker, he suffered a drink problem – now cured!) and Bobby Rondinelli was brought in. Those sessions were scrapped and new ones used in the final version of the album, featuring Rarebell. At the same time, a specially-designed giant-scorpion stage-set was scrapped – £20,000 discarded – because it wasn't right for the band, and the "Blackout" set re-vamped for their latest eight month world tour. But besides touring – and the Scorpions are true rock'n'roll gypsies, who love being on the road – they're conscious of the need to support their music with the new visual medium, the rock video, and for their 'Rock You Like A Hurricane' video hired ace producer/director David Mallet (whose work with Def Leppard and Iron Maiden was excellent) on a budget of £50,000. Mallet has also been hired for their summer single, 'Still Loving You'. It indicates the nature of the Scorpions' international success that these days they can afford to be so exacting in everything they do. In the States at present they're second only to Van Halen on the rock circuit, while worldwide their new album has won gold records. And the music? – well, the music is better than it has ever been, with new classics like 'Coming Home' joining older numbers like 'Dynamite' and 'Another Piece Of Meat' as a live favourite.

Promised for 1985 is a second double live album, recorded on their world tour and featuring material from *Lovedrive* onwards. And, according to the band, it marks the end of their second phase of development, just as *Tokyo Tapes* marked the end of their first. What lies ahead remains to be seen, but what's certain is that there'll be a few million fans waiting to find out.

Albums:

Lonesome Crow (1972)   *Fly To The Rainbow* (1974)   *In Trance* (1975)   *Virgin Killer* (1976)   *Taken By Force* (1977)   *Best Of* (1977)★   *Hot & Heavy* (1977)★   *Tokyo Tapes* (1978)   *Lovedrive* (1979)   *Animal Magnetism* (1980)   *Best 2* (1980)★   *Blackout* (1982)   *Love At First Sting* (1984)

★Compilation albums

Slade

Back in 1968 you would have found the four members of Slade touring the Wolverhampton area as The In Betweens, playing cover versions of other people's famous songs in all the local clubs. A year on and you'd have found them as Ambrose Slade, a semi-skinhead band with their own footstomping style. It was then that manager Chas Chandler 'discovered' the band, shortened its name to Slade and got them their first recording contract.

From the very start Slade have been raucous sing-along rockers with an ear for a good tune and a liking for loud and heavy music Noddy Holder (vocals and guitar), Dave Hill (guitar), Jimmy Lea (bass and piano) and Don Powell (drums) are also one of the longest-lasting stable line-ups in rock music. They are also one of the UK's most successful 'pop' groups, although they've never had a top forty single in the States (Quiet Riot did that for them recently, however!).

At a time when glitter and glam were in fashion in the UK, Slade adopted the style and transcended it – their stack heels taller than anyone else's, their hats bigger, more sparkling – whilst at the same time producing seven classic singles, six of which went to No. 1 in the UK charts: 'Coz I Luv You', 'Take Me Back 'Ome', 'Mama We're All Crazy Now', 'Cum On Feel The Noize', 'Squeeze Me, Please Me', 'Merry Xmas Everybody' and 'Gudbuy T'Jane'. Between 1972 and 1974 they dominated the British singles chart and took their energy-packed show all over the country, playing to ecstatic audiences. But by 1975 and

their seventh album, *In Flame* (the music to a film in which they starred), their star was going out, and by 1977 they could call their eighth album by the ironical title of *Whatever Happened to Slade?*

Of course, even out of the media spotlight, Slade were still playing good stomp-your-foot, nod-your-head music and still packing in their faithful crowds, but it wasn't until 1983 that they returned to the British charts with two hit singles, 'My O My' and 'Run Runaway (released in January 1984). All traces of skinhead garb or glitter had long vanished by 1983, and some of the tracks on their *The Amazing Kamikaze Syndrome* album were unabashed Heavy Metal, with no concessions to pop – 'Slam The Hammer Down', for instance. And with Quiet Riot and Mama's Boys producing hit covers of their old material, the media were beginning to pay attention again. Where had the band been? Well, one quick answer would be to hand the would-be enquirer a copy of their 1982 live album, *Slade On Stage*, one of their finest, most powerful sets, as an answer.

Slade's movement into the Heavy Metal camp is only confirming what long-standing headbangers have known all along, and the fact that Slade can be found supporting Ozzy Osbourne on his Canadian tour in 1984 only goes to prove that even after sixteen years together the band can still produce some of the most exciting heavy music about. Oh, and take a football scarf along if you go to one of their gigs; you may need it when the crowd start singing at the end!

Albums:

Beginnings (1969) *Play It Loud* (1970) *Slade Alive* (1972) *Slayed* (1972) *Sladest* (1973) *Old, New, Borrowed And Blue* (1974) *In Flame* (1975) *Whatever Happened To Slade?* (1977) *The Story Of Slade* (Germany, 1977)* *Nobody's Fools* (1978) *Slade Alive! Volume 2* (1979) *Return To Base* (1980) *Slade Smashes* (1980)* *We'll Bring The House Down* (1981) *Til Deaf Us Do Part* (1981) *Slade On Stage* (1982) *The Amazing Kamikaze Syndrome* (1983) *Keep Your Hands Off My Power Supply* (1984) *Slade's Greatz* (1984)*

* Compilation albums.

Billy Squier

Few artists have attained solo mega-stardom in the heavy metal field without first making a name for themselves within previous big-name groups: Ozzy Osbourne in Black Sabbath, Ted Nugent in the legendary Amboy Dukes, Michael Schenker in UFO, Gillan in Deep Purple, Sammy Hagar in Montrose, etc . . . Billy Squier is the exception to the rule.

His first bands were minor and his involvement with them particularly short/lived, as his ambition was always to make it on his own. Billy Squier was born in Boston, where he formed his first band, the Sidewinders, while still in his mid-teens. At the age of eighteen he joined up with a group called Piper; an album was recorded before Billy decided to go his own way, as Piper were adopting too much of a pop

approach, and Billy's taste ran more to high energy power rock.

He signed as a solo artist with Capitol and 1980 saw the release of his first album, *Tale Of The Tape*, produced by Eddie Offord, veteran of Yes and many pomp rock bands. The critics were generally good, but commercial results were disappointing, with just a minor hit in the singles charts. Squier followed up in 1981 with *Don't Say No*. This second album saw Billy sharing the production credits with Reinholdt Mack, better known as plain Mack. The combination worked, and the LP soon lodged itself in the American Top Five, thanks to three hit tunes, including 'The Stroke' which reached number 17 in the *Billboard* charts and 'In The Dark' which peaked at number 35. 'My Kinda Lover', though with less vinyl impact, is still fondly remembered for its video.

Billy Squier is thus the ultimate solo heavy metal star as he writes his own material, plays guitar in an aggressive but disciplined style chockablock with tight riffs, sings and even co-produces himself! The association with Mack continued with a third album, *Emotions In Motion* in 1982, which boasted an Andy Warhol cover and unveiled another hit with 'Everybody Wants You', the video of which is a strong concert performance devoid of thrills and dominated by the riff-led music. With his long, curly dark hair and soft looks, Billy Squier is also one of heavy metal's better-looking idols. His music is in the great British melodic tradition of Free and Led Zeppelin and many have observed similarities between his voice and that of Zeppelin's Robert Plant, and it ain't a bad comparison. Squier can certainly live with it.

Despite the album's success, Squier wasn't totally satisfied with *Emotions in Motion* and proceeded to re-mix it himself, which resulted in both a new version of the platter and a collapse due to overwork in 1982.

1983 saw Billy back on the road and contributing a track to the soundtrack of *Fast Times at Ridgemont High*, the Amy Heckerling movie about life in American high school. It has been a long wait and his fourth album, soon to be released at the time of writing, promises to be a major breakthrough with production chores handled by Jim Steinman, of the "kitchen sink and more" fame.

Albums:

Tale of the Tape (1980) *Don't Say No* (1981) *Emotions in Motion* (1982) two versions *Signs Of Life* (1984)

PHOTO: L.F.I./FRANK GRIFFIN

Status Quo

Status Quo are a British institution, like the Royal Family and cricket, and when they disband after their British/European tour in July 1984, an era will be over.

Founder members Francis Rossi (guitar/vocals) and Alan Lancaster (bass) first formed a band called the Scorpions in 1962 as thirteen-year-old schoolboys. Then as the Spectres they recruited John Coughlan on drums and recorded a few singles, adding Roy Lynes to their line-up on organ and vocals. A brief spell as Traffic Jam followed in 1967 before Rick Parfitt joined them and they changed their name to Status Quo in August 1967. Almost immediately (November 1967) they had a hit with "Pictures Of Matchstick Men', which went to No. 7 in the UK charts. The guitar and vocals of Parfitt proved a perfect comple-

ment to Rossi's boogie-based riffs. They remained a five-piece until late 1970 when Lynes left the band, recording three albums and hits like 'Ice In The Sun' and 'Down The Dustpipe'.

As a four-piece, their sound shorn of organ, their music became simpler, harder-edged and riff-dominated. Over the next twelve years they became the definitive working-class British heavy-riffing boogie band. Their 1973 album, *Piledriver*, which spawned the hit single 'Paper Plane', set the course for their music; a course to which they've unerringly steered, mixing hard rock, blues and ballads in equal measure. Further UK hits followed with 'Caroline', 'Break The Rules', 'Down Down' (their first No. 1, in 1974), and, later in the decade, 'Rockin' All Over The

World', 'Again And Again' and 'Whatever You Want'. Since *Piledriver* every one of their albums has climbed into the top five of the UK charts (*Hello, On The Level* and *Blue For You* were all No. 1 albums), yet success in the States has always evaded them, perhaps because their brand of heavy, head-banging boogie is so definitively British.

1982 saw the first line-up change in the band in a decade when John Coughlan left the band and was replaced on drums by Pete Kircher, formerly of Original Mirrors, while Andy Bown was added on keyboards for the *1982* album. It was this line-up that played a concert at the N.E.C. Hall in Birmingham, England, in front of Prince Charles and Lady Di (a performance which can be found on the last two sides of their retrospective triple album, *From The Makers Of. . .*). Status Quo as a five-piece was a return full circle to their origins. But full circle and to an end? Well, not quite, for though Quo fans will no longer have the delight of seeing Rossi, Parfitt and Lancaster lined up on stage, heads down together while the hard riffs thump from the amps, they still plan to come together from time to time to record an album. Quo are dead; long live the Quo!

Albums:
Picturesque Matchstickable Messages (1968)   *Spare Parts* (1969)   *Ma Kelly's Greasy Spoon* (1970)   *Dog Of Two Head* (1971)   *Piledriver* (1973)   *Hello* (1973)   *Quo* (1974)   *On The Level* (1975)   *Blue For You* (1976)   *Status Quo Live!* (1977)   *Rockin' All Over The World* (1977)   *If You Can't Stand The Heat* (1978)   *Whatever You Want* (1979)   *Just Supposin'* (1980)   *Never Too Late* (1981)   *1982* (1982)   *From The Makers Of . . .* (1982)   *Back To Back* (1983)

Compilations:
Status Quo-Tations (1969)   *The Best Of Status Quo* (1973)   *Golden Hour Of Status Quo* (1973)   *Down The Dustpipe* (1975)   *The Rest Of Status Quo* (1976)   *The Status Quo File* (1977)   *Status Quo* (1978)   *The Status Quo Collection* (1978)   *Just For The Record* (1979)   *Twelve Gold Bars* (1980)   *Status Quo* (1980)   *1972–1980* (France, 1980)   *Works* (1983)

38 Special

38 Special hail from Jacksonville, Florida, home of the legendary Lynyrd Skynyrd, and it's no surprise to learn that Special's lead vocalist, Donnie Van Zant, is brother of Skynyrd's Ronnie (who tragically died in a plane crash in 1977).

Formed as a six-piece in 1975, they have had only one personnel change, in 1978, when bassist Ken Lyons was replaced by Larry Junstrom. Sharing vocal credits with Van Zant is Don Barnes, who also shares lead guitar duties with Jeff Carlisi. Making up the rhythm section are the band's two drummers, Jack Grondin and Steve Brookins. With this line-up, 38 Special have released six albums, beginning with *.38 Special* in 1977, a limited local success.

On their first two albums (*Special Delivery* followed in 1978) the band seemed heavily influenced by their Southern States predecessors, the Allman Brothers Band, and, of course, Lynyrd Skynyrd. The music on these albums was good ol' Southern-fried boogie – but 38 Special didn't want to be imitators – they were tired of the cliches, though not the spirit of Southern rock – and from *Rockin' Into The Night* onward they deliberately moved away from boogie, bringing in new songwriters from outside the band. Their new music merged the old style with a more energetic form of Adult Oriented Rock, melodic but with a cutting edge of heaviness. The move was highly successful and their fourth album, *Wild-Eyed Southern Boys,* released in 1981, went platinum. Not only that, but the band began to have top thirty singles in the States, with 'Hold On Loosely' (No.27) and then, in 1982, a top ten single with 'Caught Up In You'.

The South has produced several big-selling rock acts, Molly Hatchet, Blackfoot and Doc Holliday amongst them, but 38 Special are the true survivors of the Southern music movement of the mid-seventies. But while *Special Forces* and *Tour de Force* have sold more than a million copies each in the States, earning the band more platinum discs, 38 Special (unlike, say, ZZ Top) have yet to win a solid following outside their homeland, nor have they yet chosen to tour Britain or Europe. Which is a shame, because live, 38 Special can be real show-stoppers, with Donnie Van Zant's penchant for leaping into crowds and flying across the stage in harness, and the band's general "high-octane" driving force. "We're not just whiskey-drinkin' alligator-chasin' guys", Don Barnes insists, but that doesn't mean they're not fun either. 38 Special are heavy entertainment, Southern States-style.

Albums:

38 Special (1977)   *Special Delivery* (1978)   *Rockin' Into The Night* (1979)   *Wild-Eyed Southern Boys* (1981)   *Special Forces* (1982)   *Tour De Force* (1983)

PHOTO SUPPLIED BY A & M

Pat Travers

Canadian Pat Travers was born in 1954 and, like so many guitar heroes of his generation, discovered hard rock in his early teens. From the age of twelve he played guitar, his influences being the then-emerging heavy rock guitarists like Hendrix, Beck, Clapton and Page. Amongst the early bands he played for was Red Hot, who gigged in the Quebec area. But Travers wasn't planning to stay long in local bands. He joined Merge and was spotted playing by 50s/60s rock'n'roll veteran Ronnie Hawkins, who drafted Travers into his band as lead guitarist.

Travers was a fully-fledged professional when he made his way to London in the mid-seventies. Unlike other hopefuls who had made the trek to London (Rush's Neil Peart for one), Travers was lucky enough to meet the right people and, within months, had put a band together. Drummer Nico McBrain (who went on to join French band Trust and is now in Iron Maiden) and bassist Mars Cowling (a session musician of some considerable experience) formed the first Pat Travers Band; a hard-rocking trio playing Pat Travers' own compositions. Their first outing was called simply *Pat Travers*. Released in 1976, it received a good response, even though the music press were turning away from hard rock and towards the then-developing new wave of punk.

Makin' Magic, Travers' early '77 album, was the last to feature the trio. Travers replaced McBrain with drummer Tommy Aldridge (who can now be found – intermittently – in Ozzy Osbourne's band!) and recruited guitarist Pat Thrall to broaden the band's sound. The first fruits of this new line-up appeared later in the year, with *Putting It Straight*, a more sophisticated album, and one which was a better showcase of Travers' fast but expressive guitar style.

The four-piece stayed together for a further three albums, including the excellent live set, *Go For What You Know*, where the strengths of Travers' own compositions are vividly displayed – 'Makes No Difference' is a real highlight. But the 1980 album, *Crash And Burn* was the last with Thrall and Aldridge. Travers decided to continue with a trio, and brought in drummer Sandy Gennaro. *Radio Active* was the first album to come out of this new band, and proved rather patchy – Travers experimenting with new musical forms, not always successfully. For his 1982 album, *Black Pearl,* however, Travers was back on top form, returning to the fast, hard-rocking style of earlier albums.

Travers' current band – only three of the seven musicians used on his 1984, *Hot Shot* album – is the first not to

PHOTO SUPPLIED BY POLYDOR

feature Peter 'Mars' Cowling on bass. Barry Dunaway (bass), Pat Machino (drums) and Jerry Riggs (guitar) are Travers' present back-up band – one which might, after a four-year absence from touring the UK, finally bring Travers' excellent live show back to where he started out. And with the new album even better than the last, Pat Travers seems set to end his first decade as a solo artist more popular than he's ever been.

Albums:
Pat Travers (1976) *Makin' Magic* (1977) *Putting It Straight* (1977) *Heat In The Street* (1978) *Go For What You Know* (1979) *Crash And Burn* (1980) *Radio Active* (1981) *Black Pearl* (1982) *Hot Shot* (1984)

Triumph

Like Rush and Led Zeppelin before them, Triumph balance their music somewhere between acoustic delicacy and heavy metal assault. 'Pomp Rock', some critics have called it: well-scripted, melodic rock which depends upon contrasts and dynamics for its impact. And, like Rush and Zeppelin, Triumph are virtuosi, in full command of their broad pallet of sound. This isn't to say, however, that Triumph are derivative, it's simply an attempt at categorising whereabouts on the musical spectrum the band lies.

Triumph were formed in 1975, in Toronto, Canada (home of Rush), and released their first album, *Triumph*, in 1976. Rick Emmett is their guitarist and shares lead vocals with Gil Moore, the band's drummer. On bass and keyboards is Mike Levine. It's a stable and seemingly unchangeable line-up, with all three contributing to the songwriting.

Triumph was an intriguing debut, with orchestrated pieces like 'Blinding Light Show' (with its soft acoustic passages) and out-and-out rockers like 'Street Fighter'; a blend (the first from Emmett, the second from Moore) which was to remain a constant in their albums. In 1977 came *Rock 'N' Roll Machine* which, curiously enough, became a big hit in Texas (a surprise because it was, like *Triumph*, issued only in Canada). On the strength of that Triumph headlined a brief tour of the Lone Star state, came to the attention of RCA and were signed up.

Triumph have always put a lot into their live shows – lighting, strobes, flashes, massive flame-machines, lasers and high-tech instrumentation. They've their own recording studios, Metalworks, in Toronto, and both Emmett and Levine are production experts. This expertise has given Triumph an edge, in that their live act has a gloss few bands achieve. This live excitement was given its first airing shortly after RCA had signed the band, when they took their show to 24 US cities on a major tour. It was a great success, and helped boost sales of *Just A Game*, their 1978 album.

Each album has shown a distinct progression from the last. 1979's *Progression Of Power*, platinum in their home country, was a lavishly produced affair with a cutting edge, and the single from it, 'Hold On', reached No. 38 in the US charts in August that year. Triumph fans had to wait for the follow-up album to *Progressions* until 1982, when *Allied Forces* emerged, packed by a massive US/Canadian tour, the "Allied Forces Trek", filmed for a video.

The fact that the best is to come from Triumph was confirmed with the release of *Never Surrender*, in 1983 (again backed by a tour – this time extending to Europe). Beside the expected acoustic/virtuosi tracks (like 'A Minor Prelude') there are hard rockers like 'All The Way'. The tour, scheduled for the Autumn, will be their biggest (and grandest in terms of production) yet, and a live album is to be recorded on the road. After the last two albums both the new releases should be well worth waiting for.

Albums:

Triumph (1976) *Rock 'N' Roll Machine* (1977) *Triumph* (1978)* *Just A Game* (1978) *Progressions Of Power* (1979) *Allied Forces* (1982) *Never Surrender* (1983)

* Compilation of first two albums.

Twisted Sister

Twisted Sister emerged some time around 1982, which is not to say that they didn't exist as a band before then, simply that 1982 was when it all happened for the band, who have been described as the world's ugliest group, and (by themselves) as "just a bunch of dirtbags".

Twisted Sister's lead singer and outrageous publicist is Dee Snider, who is supposed to have formed his first band when he was just seven. Like all the members of the band, he was a tough, street-wise New York kid. Nowadays they're no less street-wise, no less outrageous; in fact, outrage is a key factor in Twisted Sister's act, if not in their off-stage lives.

Dee Snider first met Jay Jay French (guitars) and Eddie Ojeda in 1976. French had been in NY band Wicked Lester (half of which went on to form Kiss!). Then, in 1978, bassist Mark 'The Animal' Mendoza joined the embryonic Twisted Sister from the Dictators, and the present all-fun package was completed early in 1982 when drummer AJ Pero joined. But times were lean in the States for the band and they came to England, playing the Reading Festival and a whole series of gigs about the country. In no time at all they had built themselves a fanatical UK following, who recognized that Twisted Sister had more energy in their live act than any other three bands put together. UFO's Peter Way produced their first album, *Under The Blade*, that year, but after their gutsy live show it was a great disappointment. Better was their appearance on TV's *The Tube* in the UK. It was a great evening, and an Atlantic Records executive signed the band on the strength of their performance.

The band's first album for their new label, *You Can't Stop Rock'N'Roll* was a vast improvement on their debut and sold more that 200,000 copies in the States by word of mouth alone. But it had been their UK fans that had kept Twisted Sister going – in the States they were more often than not mistaken for a British band – and it was in the UK that they concentrated their attention, appearing at the big Castle Donington festival in 1983 to promote their new album and pushing their single, 'I Am (I'm Me)' into the UK charts through guest appearances on BBC's 'Top Of The Pops' show – one of the few heavy metal bands to break into that market.

Their third album, *Stay Hungry*, was the first recorded in the States, and at last the band seem to be turning to their homeland, playing a much more sophisticated

PHOTO: REX FEATURES

(though no less heavy) form of Adult-Oriented Rock. But if the album is more polished, perhaps more accessible, their live show is still something *not* to be missed, if only to see Dee and the boys parading in their garish make-up, like some dowdy transvestite with the hots.

Albums:
Under The Blade (1982) You Can't Stop Rock'N'Roll (1983) Stay Hungry (1984)

UFO

It's hard to believe that one of the greatest cult bands in heavy metal, and, until its demise last year, one of the longest-running heavy rock groups, recorded its first album part-time in six evenings back in March 1970 for £400 – an album which made no impact on the British market whatsoever.

In August 1969, Pete Way (bass), Phil Mogg (vocals) and Mick Bolton (guitar), who had been playing in a North London band, Hocus Pocus, linked up with drummer Andy Parker and formed UFO. By March the next year they had signed with Beacon Records and their first album, the much under-rated *UFO 1,* was released soon afterwards. And suddenly the band were rock stars. They had two top ten singles, a hit album, and were headlining a nationwide tour . . . in Japan.

In the last decade Japan has become renowned for its excellent treatment of those heavy metal heroes neglected in their home countries. They've recognized many a prophet of the axe long before those heroes' homelands have embraced them – as Gary Moore, for one, will testify – but UFO began it all fourteen years ago.

Flying (sometimes known as "One Hour Space Rock", a good description of the album's contents), followed in 1971, which, like the debut album, was interesting but flawed; UFO had yet to find their own "voice". Even so it was another hit – in Japan, Germany and France. And a live album, recorded specially for the Japanese market, *UFO: Landed in Japan,* was much heavier and gave an indication of their future direction.

In February 1972 the band eased out guitarist Bolton and brought in ex-Blodwyn Pigg man, Larry Wallis. This line-up lasted all of ten months, then Wallis was out (to join the Pink Fairies) and Bernie Marsden was in. Germany loved the new band, but Britain still ignored them. They

dallied with 'glitter', then the rage in the UK, but in June 1973 they lost Marsden to Wild Turkey. Two years had passed without an album or single – without, in fact, a recording deal of any kind.

It was June 1973 and UFO were still quite popular in Germany. Michael Schenker, guitarist for a small German rock group (!), the Scorpions, had just joined the band in place of Marsden (the band's fourth guitarist in as many years!). This line-up persuaded Chrysalis to sign them and recorded the impressive *Phenomenon* album, released in May 1974. It was hard, heavy, driving and . . . it sold in Britain. Tracks like 'Doctor Doctor' and 'Rock Bottom', stage favourites for years to come, got radio play. And, most important of all, the band launched its first headlining tour of the UK. Schenker stayed and the band recruited ex-Skid Row guitarist Paul Chapman to broaden their sound, but Chapman went the way of (almost) all previous guitarists and *Force It,* the fifth UFO album, was recorded by the four-piece. Released in July 1975, it was a minor chart success in the States, following the band's tour there.

The band still felt they needed a richer sound, though, and for the *No Heavy Petting* album they brought in Danny Peyronel on keyboards. But the classic UFO line-up was formed in July 1976 when Paul Raymond came into the band as second guitarist. With this line-up (minus Peyronel) the band recorded *Lights Out* (No.23 in the US charts), *Obsession* (No.26 in the UK) and *Strangers In The Night,* an excellent double live set which reached No.7 in the UK charts. At long last UFO were big worldwide; but Schenker was restless, and in November 1978 he left to rejoin the Scorpions. Paul Chapman of Lone Star came in as his replacement, staying until the group's demise in 1983.

The new line-up was every bit as popular as the old, and their 1980 album, *No Place To Run,* reached No.11 in the UK charts. But then Raymond, whose keyboard and guitar work had given the band much of its late seventies feel, left to join Schenker in MSG, and Neil Carter of Wild Horses was brought in, This band, with its unchanged, and seemingly unchangeable, core of Way, Mogg and Parker, had two top twenty albums in the UK and was a huge crowd-puller in the States (where their albums were regularly in the top 100 of the charts). But June 1982 saw this core split when Pete Way left to form his own band, Waysted. UFO drafted in Paul Gray on bass and carried on for another year, releasing their parting shot, *Making Contact,* before calling it a day.

Never simply a heavy band, UFO blended superb heavy riffing with melodic harmonies (listen to 'Doing It All For You' on *Mechanix,* for instance) and were constantly developing throughout their history. The fourteen albums they've left are a reflection not merely of the band's maturation but of the maturation of their chosen musical form, Heavy Metal, in the seventies and early eighties.

Albums:

UFO 1 (1970)   *Flying* (1971)   *UFO: Landed In Japan* (1971)   *Phenomenon* (1974)   *Force It* (1975)   *No Heavy Petting* (1976)   *Lights Out* (1977)   *Strangers In The Night* (1978)   *Obsessions* (1978)   *No Place To Run* (1979)   *The Wild, The Willing, And The Innocent* (1981)   *Mechanix* (1982)   *Headstone: The Best Of UFO* (1983)*   *Making Contact* (1983)

* Compilation.

Van Halen

They've made the Guinness Book of Records as the most expensive rock band under the sun after they were paid one and a half million dollars for playing at the US Festival in 1983 – that's sixteen thousand dollars per minute. Dave Lee Roth, the pouting, charismatic singer has taken out a paternity insurance with Lloyds of London to ensure a carefree enjoyment of life on the road. Eddie Van Halen's guitar solo on Michael Jackson's 'Beat It" is credited with propelling Jackson into his present mega-platinum status. Van Halen are the band that legends are made of!

Alex and Eddie Van Halen were ten and eight years old when their parents, Jan and Eugenia Van Halen, decided to move to America. Jan was a jazz musician while Eugenia was of Indonesian descent, and the only thing they brought with them to the USA was a piano. Alex and Eddie both studied piano for sixteen years, but soon picked up on drums and guitar. In 1973, the two brothers enrolled at Pasadena City College to study music theory. Here, in the music department, they met up with Michael Anthony, then a trumpet player who also played bass. David Lee Roth, whose family had moved from Indiana to California was taking theatre courses at the same school. The two brothers were then playing in a small band called Mammoth and Dave was singing with the local Red Ball Jets, and Mike Anthony was with Snake. Impressed by each other's playing and ambition, they formed a new

outfit which they were initially going to call Rat Salade, but Dave prevailed and Van Halen was the chosen moniker.

From the outset, Dave proved a flamboyant frontman, deliberately going over the top to grab the necessary attention while the other guys cultivated their musicianship. Attracting much local following, with their electric brand of mayhem in great demand at wet t-shirt contests, they were soon booked into the prestigious Los Angeles Starwood Club, where they caught the attention of Gene Simmons of Kiss (then in their heyday). He was so impressed by the young band that he financed their first demo tapes; unfortunately, his management remained unimpressed and refused to take Van Halen on. Shortly thereafter, Warner Bros. executive Ted Templeman made the journey to the Starwood and quickly signed them up. He also became their producer and has remained so to this day.

The first album was released in 1978 and its first single, a fiery reworking of the Kinks' 'You Really Got Me' reached number 36 in the charts while the album proceeded to sell two million copies. Van Halen were here to stay, and their career never deviated thereafter from its still-rising upward curve.

All their following albums, *Van Halen II, Women and Children First, Fair Warning* and *Diver Down* achieved platinum status with comparative ease while spawning hit singles like 'Dance the Night Away' (number 15), 'Pretty Woman' (the old Roy Orbison goldie, revamped with a loud vengeance – number 12) and 'Dancing in the Street' (number 38).

Each of the albums was a careful blend of well-known past hits with a new metallic veneer of guitar and vocal virtuosity and self-penned originals from the band, but *1984*, their last album witnessed a determination to progress further with an all-original set and Eddie Van Halen taking tentative steps on synthesiser. The experiment was wildly successful, giving the band their first chart-topping single, 'Jump', and the album peaked at number two,

ironically just behind Michael Jackson's *Thriller*, which Eddie's guitar licks had done so much to break through to a larger, white, public.

Van Halen on stage are a truly unique experience. The charismatic Dave Lee Roth is an ebullient and outrageous front personality whose strong vocals are overshadowed by his spectacular histrionics and attire. Clad in the tightest possible leather and/or spandex, his golden mane ever in motion as he leaps about, he alternates sword play theatrics with breathtaking triple-somersault acrobatics and, literally, plays himself like an instrument. In the flesh, however, Roth proves a highly articulate and humorous personality, quite aware of his image and trading upon it quite shamelessly. Van Halen on the road leave a wake of wild parties and wrecked rooms behind them.

Master guitar player Eddie Van Halen is a shy and studious guy, happily married to soap opera actress Valerie Bertinelli, he never has enough rehearsal or playing time and can always be found guitar in hand, experimenting away in his portable studio. It is said by many that Eddie is the true heir to Jimi Hendrix as the prominent axe wizard of the 80s and, indeed, his searing, spiralling hard-rock licks have provided a new sense of excitement to heavy metal music.

Although often slagged by critics, Van Halen's success is a popular one. They are the embodiment of everything rock 'n' roll is about: fast-living, adrenalin pumping, volume and gaudiness.

"It's about what everybody feels on a Friday or Saturday night, says bass player Michael Anthony, explaining the Van Halen lifestyle "You come home from work or school, you have your bath, you shave, you jump in your car, you pick up your girlfriend and you're gonna have a good time. Well, with Van Halen every night's a Saturday night."

Albums:
Van Halen (1978) *Van Halen II* (1979) *Women and Children First* (1980) *Fair Warning* (1981) *Diver Down* (1982) *1984* (1984)

Whitesnake

When singer Ian Gillan left Deep Purple in early 1973 the band approached several 'name' vocalists for a replacement, but without success. Then, anonymously, they advertised in *Melody Maker's* band columns and sifted through the resultant bag full of tapes to see whether there was anyone worth auditioning. One of those tapes had been sent in by a young sales assistant from a boutique in Redcar, Yorkshire, a part-time singer in a band called The Fabulosa Brothers. His name was David Coverdale. Deep Purple auditioned him, hired him and, in the next two and a half years featured him on three studio albums, *Burn, Stormbringer* and *Come Taste The Band*, as well as two live offerings. From total obscurity, Coverdale was suddenly an internationally-acclaimed rock star, imitated just as much as his predecessor Gillan had been by aspiring singers.

Then, when Purple split, Coverdale was caught in the contractual hassles of the breakup and prevented from playing live. The prestige of fronting Deep Purple, one of the world's biggest-earning acts did, however, allow him to release two solo albums (on Purple Records), *White Snake* in 1977, and *North Winds* in 1978. But Coverdale was dissatisfied with "making music in his own front room" and acutely missed the joys and tensions of touring. The first solo album had used session musicians, including an old friend, Mick Moody, on lead guitar, whom Coverdale had met at a Middlesbrough art college years before. The second solo album kept Moody for guitar, but brought in Bernie Marsden as second guitarist, with David 'Duck' Dowle on drums, Brian Johnson on keyboards and ex-National Health and Colloseum II bassist, Neil Murray. It was this band which toured in February 1978 under the title of "David Coverdale's Whitesnake". But punk was at its height, and long-haired rockers weren't the flavour of the month, so the tour was low-key in its choice of venues. The band, playing a mixture of R & B, Blues and Soul, mixed up and made heavy, made its debut at Nottingham's Sky Bird Club on 23 February 1978, and from the first got a good response from the fans. They toured with the Police around this time, then signed with United Artists.

When Brian Johnson quit the band, Pete Solley was brought in on keyboards but left shortly afterwards, being replaced by Coverdale's old 'guvnor' at Deep Purple, Jon Lord. It was this line-up that recorded the first proper Whitesnake album (the "David Coverdale's Whitesnake" tag had been dropped by this stage), *Trouble*, in London during that summer. The album was a curious mixture of things but did (despite its opening number, 'Take Me With You') manage to keep away from sounding like Deep Purple, mainly through its fast-blues emphasis. Then, when David Dowle left, and ex-Purple drummer Ian Paice

stepped in, the media *did* begin to call Whitesnake 'Purple in disguise'. It was an accusation which the second group album, *Lovehunter*, released in October 1979, should have dispelled. Whitesnake were heavy, yes, but they were much bluesier than Purple had ever been and Moody's guitar style (cultivated in groups like Tramline, Juicy Lucy and SNAFU) was nothing like Ritchie Blackmore's.

Talking of Ritchie Blackmore . . . Since Whitesnake's inception they have always suffered from continual comparisons with Ritchie Blackmore's Rainbow. Critics have loved to play Coverdale off against Blackmore in a battle of the egos, recalling the clashes the two reputedly had in Purple, and there's an element of truth in this, to the extent that Coverdale scuffled with Blackmore in Zurich in 1980 after one of Blackmore's perennial practical jokes was aimed at Coverdale's German wife, Julia.

In any case, Whitesnake weren't a one-guitar band, and Bernie Marsden's playing, as much as Mick Moody's, went to create Whitesnake's hard R & B sound (Marsden's own pedigree is UFO, Wild Turkey, Babe Ruth and Paice, Ashton, Lord). Whitesnake play what Coverdale has called "cock rock"; the stark sexual imagery which makes them so unpopular with women's libbers makes them oh so popular with their fans, male and female alike. This emphasis is reflected in the title of their third album, *Ready An' Willing*, which reached No. 6 in the UK charts in May 1980. But before that, in October 1979, Whitesnake had released an EP. *Long Way From Home*, which

included the beautiful blues number, 'Ain't No Love In The Heart Of The City' (listen to the crowd sing the chorus to this on the live album!), and a single, 'Fool For Your Loving' which climbed the charts in April 1980, paving the way for the album the following month. But Whitesnake live were something different, as the live double album, *Live . . . In The Heart Of The City*, released in October 1980, proved. Two sides were of the band in November 1978, two of their recent June 1980 concerts – all at the Hammersmith Odeon – and it's interesting to compare the two versions of 'Come On' (the show-opener) to gauge the band's development. If Whitesnake weren't as popular as Deep Purple worldwide, their British following was beginning to match Purple's in size and fanaticism.

Come An' Get It appeared in April 1981, the same immaculate blues-rock mixture which spawned two moderately successful singles, 'Don't Break My Heart 'Again' and 'Would I Lie To You'. Once again there was that emphasis on hard lovin' men and satisfied women (though listen to 'Girl'). The band was playing better than ever, and tours of Europe, Japan and the States widened their audience, yet somehow worldwide success evaded them – they seemed forever on the verge.

In late 1982 the sixth Whitesnake album, *Saints An' Sinners* appeared and went to No. 9 in the UK charts. Mel Galley (who had been in Trapeze with ex-Deep Purple bassist, Glenn Hughes) provided backing vocals, and later joined the band full-time, replacing Bernie Marsden on lead guitar. This wasn't the only shakeup in the Whitesnake line-up that occured at this time. Neil Murray, for a long time uncomfortable in the band, left, being replaced by Colin 'bomber' Hodgkinson, and on drums Cozy Powell came in (ironically, after an earlier spell in Rain-

bow!) to replace Ian Paice. Mel Galley was, by this time, co-writing most of the band's material with Coverdale, and the result of their labours was the much-delayed *Slide It In*, released in early 1984.

The new album was worth the wait, and the first side of the album particularly was classic Whitesnake music. But the end of 1983 had seen Mick Moody leave the band after seven years' service, to be replaced in January '84 by ex-Thin Lizzy axeman, John Sykes. At the same time Neil Murray was back, reconciled to the group and replacing Hodgkinson. Then, in May, Jon Lord announced that he was quitting the group to join the re-formed Deep Purple. The rumours had been circulating for same while and various names had been cited as possible replacements, but in the end Coverdale decided to continue the group without a regular organist. This much-changed (and yet, in Heavy Metal terms, quite familiar) line-up toured the States in the summer of 1984, supporting the Scorpions, still seeking that evasive break-through. Will they? Who knows . . . One thing's for sure, though; it'll be a gross injustice if they fail.

Albums:
David Coverdale:
White Snake (1977)   *North Winds* (1978)

Whitesnake:
Trouble (1978)   *Lovehunter* (1979)   *Ready An' Willing* (1980)   *Live – In The Heart Of The City* (1980)   *Come An' Get It* (1981)   *Saints An' Sinners* (1982)   *Slide It In* (1984)
(also:– *Snakebite, 1978, Holland* – a compilation Coverdale/Whitesnake album).

Y & T

If you think Y & T's career in the musical big time began with the aptly-named *Earthshaker* album in 1981, then you're wrong, but finding out about their earlier phase – as Yesterday And Today (the title of an early Yes song, incidentally!) – is difficult. Both of their early albums, *Yesterday And Today* and *Struck Down* have been deleted for some while, and unless you were following the four-piece from Oakland, California since its early days in the late seventies, then you'll only know about Y & T, the abbreviated, hard-rocking band who signed with A & M in 1981.

Earthshaker was dedicated to "all our fans of Yesterday and Today", but was unquestionably rooted more in today's music than in the softer rock of yesterday. Their A & M debut was (apparently) crisper, tougher and much, much heavier than its predecessors and had on it two undeniable heavy metal classics in 'Rescue Me' and the lengthy 'I Believe In You'. It remains their heaviest album and perhaps their best – after all, it was three years in preparation.

Y & T's move into the Heavy Metal sphere was warmly welcomed by both fans and critics. Y & T have never been a major headliner in the Kiss/Van Halen league, but they are one of Heavy Metal's most respected bands. Their second (Y & T) album, *Black Tiger* (recorded in England) appeared in 1982, and the band toured widely, appearing at the Castle Donington Festival in England and the Pink Pop Festival in Holland, then headlining tours of Britain and Japan. The high point of their year came in September, though, when they supported AC/DC on a two-month tour of Britain and a month's tour of Europe.

And who *are* Y & T? The line-up on *Earthshaker* has remained stable to this day, with Joey Alves on electric and acoustic guitars, David Maniketti on lead guitar and lead vocals, Phil Kennemore on bass, and Leonard Haze on drums.

1983 saw the band concentrating on the States where they recorded their next album, *Mean Streak*. It proved something of a disappointment after the first two albums, the sophisticated production work seeming to rob Y & T of the attractive spontaneous feel that was on the earlier cuts. Even so, tracks like 'Midnight In Tokyo' and 'Mean Streak' were powerful live numbers, proving that the band had not lost its way. 1983 also saw the band recording their

first promotional videos (including a ten-minute interview on MTV to promote the *Mean Streak* album), and planning a concept album, "Rock'N'Roll's Gonna Save The World", working with top songwriter Geoff Levy. It was to feature "Y & T man", a half-beast, half-human superhero. When it emerged, in July 1984, it was *In Rock We Trust,* featuring the previous "title" track as its opening number. Once again Y & T were concentrating their touring energies on the USA in 1984, but they did make one important UK appearance, at the Castle Donington Festival in August, before returning to their Stateside trek, supporting the newly reformed Aerosmith and promoting the new single, 'Lipstick And Leather'.

Albums:
Yesterday And Today (1976)   *Struck Down* (1978)
Earthshaker (1981)   *Black Tiger* (1982)   *Mean Streak* (1983)   *In Rock We Trust* (1984)

ZZ Top

Take three hard-nosed hombres who are into drag-racing, women and blues-based boogie, put them in ten-gallon hats, mechanics overalls, and let two of those three sport eighteen inch beards (the third is *called* Beard!), then cook for fourteen years at a high temperature. What you get is an all-Texan band called ZZ Top, formed in 1970 when Billy Gibbons (ex-Moving Sidewalk, and called by Hendrix the most promising upcoming American guitarist) asked bass guitarist Dusty Hill and drummer Frank Beard to join him in a new band. Both Hill and Beard had been in the Dallas band American Blues, but from the start it seemed as if the ZZ Top trio had been playing together years. Live, their highly choreographed, almost telepathic rapport makes it seem sometimes as if they're sharing a single co-ordinating mind as they start and stop, change musical direction or launch into a fast-paced shuffle – one of their famous boogie workouts.

Their first album, called, with startling originality, *ZZ Top's First Album*, appeared in 1971. It attracted some interest, but moderate sales, and only by touring, as support to bands like the Rolling Stones, Alice Cooper and Ten Years After did the band really make an impact on the record-buying public. Their second album, *Rio Grande Mud* received greater attention when it was released in 1972, and their third album, the delightful *Tres Hombres* went platinum in the States on its release in 1973. It was a powerful mixture of blues, R & B and heavy rock, and a single from the album, 'La Grange' (about an infamous Texan whorehouse) was a big hit.

The part-studio, part-live album, *Fandango* appeared in 1975 and proved the second platinum-seller for the band, spawning their "pussy-chasing" single, 'Tush', a hit at the time and a standard bring-the-house-down number in their live set.

ZZ Top are Texan to the core and when, in 1976/77, they launched the World Wide Texas Tour (complete with a stage-set shaped like the Lone Star State and containing cattle, snakes and buzzards) they attracted a total of 1.2 million people to come and see their little slice of 'Tejas'. *Tejas* was the album promoted on the tour and proved another big-seller, followed in 1977 by the retrospective *Best Of ZZ Top*.

After their 1978 album, *Deguello* (from which came the classic cut, 'Cheap Sunglasses') the band rested for several

years, returning in 1981 with their sixth album, *El Loco*. ZZ Top had developed from their Southern blues-boogie roots and were a much heavier band in the 80s with a tighter feel to their music. Their 1983 album, *Eliminator* was clear evidence of this movement towards a far greater sophistication. Yet none of their drive, their power, has been lost in the process. ZZ Top can still 'shuffle' with the very best of the hard-boogie bands, even though they've added synthesisers and electronics to their rock armoury.

Albums:

ZZ Top's First Album (1971) *Rio Grande Mud* (1972) *Tres Hombres* (1973) *Fandango* (1975) *Tejas* (1976) *Best Of ZZ Top* (1977)* *Deguello* (1979) *El Loco* (1981) *Eliminator* (1983)

* Compilation album.